PRAISE FOR IWAN DIETSCHI AND MASTERING HOSPITALITY

"I have long valued Iwan Dietschi's leadership, his ability to inspire others, and his commitment to his guests, staff, and the enduring values of true hospitality. In his excellent book, he guides young and established hoteliers alike to create their own pathway to success and calls on all professionals, including senior leaders, to reflect on their responsibility to continually evolve and strengthen their vision, capabilities, and example of excellence."

HERVE HUMLER
Founding member and Chairman Emeritus, The Ritz-Carlton Hotel Company and former President and Chief Operating Officer of Bulgari Hotels & Resorts and St. Regis Hotels & Resorts

"Iwan Dietschi is a true master of the art of hospitality. Through his own story, his 5-star career journey, and his wide experience leading others, he shows the value of being true to yourself while always putting people first. With heart and practical guidance, he lays out an 8-step path anyone in the "business of people" can follow to achieve one's goals and create a career with purpose."

HOWARD BEHAR,
Former president of Starbucks
and author of *It's Not About the Coffee*

"Iwan Dietschi embodies the passion of hospitality. As part of the 8 Principles in *Mastering Hospitality*, I am thrilled that he highlights the importance of lifetime learning, especially self-directed. The eternal enquiring mind makes for a more satisfied professional who is also better able to interpret today's changing consumer demands."

MARY GOSTELOW
Gostelow Report and GirlAhead, and Global Ambassador, International Luxury Travel Market

"Driven by passion and true caring, Iwan's wonderful guide, *Mastering Hospitality*, will help all current and future hoteliers achieve leadership excellence and maintain the quality and brilliance that are required in a 5-star world."

ANDREA SCHERZ
Owner and Managing Director, Gstaad Palace, Switzerland

"A must-read for all who seek to advance and be a leader in the hospitality field. Drawing on Dr. Iwan Dietschi's proven leadership that has inspired so many, *Mastering Hospitality* demystifies the best practices of hospitality and offers readers the most compelling view of what it means to be a master hotelier."

DR. RONALD BLACK
Contributing Faculty, DBA Program, College of Management and Technology, Walden University

"As a seasoned hotelier, I have admired Iwan for his endless empathy, indisputable expertise, and incredible accomplishments. In *Mastering Hospitality*, Iwan Dietschi takes readers on his fascinating journey of becoming a superstar in the world of luxury hotels. It is an indispensable chef-d'oeuvre for anyone seeking success in the service industry in general or the hotel business in particular. Learn from the best to become the best!"

DR. ANNE-MARIE DE SCHEEMAECKER
Group CFO, IGC Group, Antwerp, Belgium

"Iwan Dietschi is an expert on leadership and luxury with an enormous talent for creativity, which makes him a unique leader in our industry. I have followed his brilliant Ritz-Carlton career and am delighted to endorse his new book, which shares the fruit of years of experience."

PIERRE PERUSSET
General Manager, The Ritz-Carlton, Hong Kong

MASTERING HOSPITALITY

A LUXURY HOTELIER'S GUIDE TO
CAREER AND LEADERSHIP SUCCESS

IWAN DIETSCHI
"DR. HOTELIER"

MASTERING HOSPITALITY

A LUXURY HOTELIER'S GUIDE TO CAREER AND LEADERSHIP SUCCESS

DIETSCHI PRESS

Copyright © 2021 by Iwan Dietschi
www.drhotelier.com

All rights reserved.

No part of this book may be reproduced or transmitted in any form or by any means, electronic or mechanical, including photocopying, recording, video, or by any information or retrieval system, without prior written permission from the publisher except for the use of brief quotations in a book review.

Published in the United States by Dietschi Press

ISBN 978-0-9894912-5-9 (hardcover)
ISBN 978-0-9894912-6-6 (paperback)
ISBN 978-0-9894912-7-3 (eBook)
ISBN 978-0-9894912-8-0 (audiobook)

For information about quantity sales, rights, and other inquiries, contact info@drhotelier.com

Cover design by PearCreative.ca
Book design by PearCreative.ca

Printed in the United States of America

DEDICATION

To my late beloved father, Josef Dietschi-Borer, my role model and mentor, who always supported me in everything I wanted to achieve. He dedicated his life to his family, and inspired people through his incredible heart, love, and selfless pursuit to do good for others.

CONTENTS

INTRODUCTION
The Beautiful Profession of the People Business 7

PART ONE
Charting a Path for Success in the Hospitality and People Business 13

    CHAPTER ONE
    My Personal Story:
    A Journey of a Lifetime 15

    CHAPTER TWO
    The History of the Hotel Business:
    A Rich Heritage 35

    CHAPTER THREE
    The Experience of Hospitality:
    The Guest Experience 47

    CHAPTER FOUR
    The Role of Hotelier:
    Being a True Host 69

    CHAPTER FIVE
    The Path to Success:
    Achieving Your Dream Career 99

PART TWO
The Eight Principles for Excellence in the People Business 119

    CHAPTER SIX
    Introducing the Eight Principles 121

    CHAPTER SEVEN
    Principle #1:
    Become Your Own Personal Brand 127

    CHAPTER EIGHT
    Principle #2:
    Define Your Vision and Mission 139

CHAPTER NINE
Principle #3:
Understand Your Company's Culture and Values   149

CHAPTER TEN
Principle #4:
Strengthen Your Personal Attributes of Hospitality   159

CHAPTER ELEVEN
Principle #5:
Build and Solidify Your Core Competencies   169

CHAPTER TWELVE
Principle #6:
Learn to Communicate Effectively   191

CHAPTER THIRTEEN
Principle #7:
Develop Your Leadership Style and Strengths   205

CHAPTER FOURTEEN
Principle #8:
Expand Your Knowledge Through Continuous Education   223

Final Words   239

Endnotes   243

Index   247

About the Author   261

Everybody can be great, because everybody can serve. You don't have to have a college degree to serve. You don't have to make your subject and your verb agree to serve... You only need a heart full of grace, a soul generated by love.

—Martin Luther King, Jr.

ACKNOWLEDGMENTS

I would like to express my deep gratitude to all my colleagues, past and present, and to everyone who influenced me positively to become a better human being and a consummate professional. I am blessed to know so many wonderful people—professionals, colleagues, friends, and in particular, all the great leaders I had the pleasure of working with. Many people made me better simply because I had their time. Most of them created their own legacies in the business, and everyone who touched my heart was not only a mentor but became a true role model and succeeded in their own career and what they wanted to achieve. These wonderful human beings have not only helped me improve but also touched the hearts and minds of so many others around the world.

I thank my company leaders, who supported me and gave me the opportunity to achieve my professional dreams, and my co-workers, with whom I had the pleasure of working and learning. I am grateful for the almost seven years of graduate study I undertook and the faculty and colleagues who taught me so much about business and industries from around the world. The passion they showed to improve themselves created better opportunities and helped others achieve their own full potential.

The big lesson for me is that we work hard for ourselves, but at the same time, we elevate others through our approach to excellence, day in and day out.

It is important for me to say a big thank-you as well to all the guests I had the pleasure to meet during my career. I learned a lot from them, and I will continue to grow through them every day.

My first and most important mentor was my late father, who was a model of humility and accessibility. He was always there to listen, to coach, and to teach my brother and me. Like most fathers, he had only our best interests at heart. Feedback, input, and discussions were open and honest at all times, even when something was not what I wanted to hear. This candor is crucial in a mentor: someone who really tells you how it is, with only your best interest in mind. Thank you so very much, my dearest Papi!

I also want to thank my wonderful Mami, Hedy Dietschi-Borer, for her love, care, and dedication to me and my brother. She always believed in me and my passion for hospitality. She assisted me with everything I needed to pursue my dreams and to achieve the best in my professional and academic life.

My incredible brother, Josef Jun, has taught me how to focus on my goals, always helped me to become better and to think out of the box, and has never stopped believing in me. He continually teaches and coaches me about how to "connect the dots."

I have the best family, and I owe everything to them. I love them very much.

ACKNOWLEDGMENTS

It is important for me to acknowledge particular people who've helped me with this book. Apart from my loved ones, who always assisted and supported me, there is a particular person I would like to mention. She is a wonderful human being, a musician, a writer, and a blogger. Ms. Leigh Ann Lombardo-Davis has been a fabulous help with this book. She is someone who experienced hardship in her life but has always remained positive about her personal concerns, and many people learned from her through reading her columns. I know she will touch the hearts of many who suffer with ill health, and she will be an angel who can bring calm and peace to their healing. Her generous sharing of her views and her writing assistance helped me enormously to articulate my ideas as I wrote the initial drafts of this manuscript.

A very special thank-you goes to Janet Goldstein, who has been the key person helping and guiding me through the editorial process as well as creating the publishing vision for my book. Her mastery and experience allowed me to achieve this important milestone.

Also many thanks to Betsy Thorpe, who assisted with the entire text; book designer Yvonne Parks at PearCreative.ca, who brought her artistic skill to the book inside and out; and Annette Leach, who ably managed the publishing process. The whole team deserves huge praise for allowing me to see my book become a reality. I could not have done it without you.

INTRODUCTION
THE BEAUTIFUL PROFESSION OF THE PEOPLE BUSINESS

This book is about my journey and lessons learned in the world's most beautiful profession—the people business. I have studied, practiced, and taught the art of being a hotelier for almost thirty years, having the wonderful fortune to spend most of my career in increasing leadership roles at one of the most renowned hotel companies in the world, The Ritz-Carlton, a brand by Marriott International.

My rewarding path and success have been shaped by amazing mentors and teachers. Now, in turn, I want to share with you the wisdom I've received and the hard-earned practical experience I've gained so you too can achieve your full potential as a leader in the hotel industry, the people business, and beyond. The personal characteristics of hospitality at the highest level—integrity, humbleness, charisma, diplomacy, curiosity, patience—are applicable and important to anyone in any field of business or industry around the world. And so are the universal leadership principles that I've honed in the hospitality business—understanding and aligning with a brand, creating welcoming environments, leading and inspiring employees, and being a formal and informal role model for others. I believe these lessons will serve anyone, at any level of seniority, who seeks to put ideas into action to reach their full potential as a professional and a leader.

From the beginning of my work as a hotelier, I have been guided by curiosity and a desire to create and live excellence, and I have always had a difficult time accepting the status quo. I have wondered how businesses and, in particular, hotels, operate in challenging market environments and why standards vary so much from hotel to hotel, by brand, and in countries around the world.

In my relentless drive for perfection and for creating a better today than yesterday, I always ask myself:

- What is the purpose of a hotel?
- What makes people want to stay at a particular hotel, and what makes them want to come back?
- What can I do—and what can we do—to create environments where everyone thrives, grows, and profits from our efforts?

Over the years, I've tried to find answers to these questions through my daily work, through travel and continuing education, including an executive MBA and later a doctorate to enhance my understanding of management and leadership at the highest level and by living and working in thirteen countries on four continents around the globe.

In this book you will learn about my personal path to success, from my humble beginnings as a business apprentice, working at the front door of my first hotel, at the front desk, then in the restaurants, attending the Lausanne Hotel School in Switzerland, and working my way up in different management positions. My first job internationally was as a housekeeping manager, and then I worked in other management positions around the world. In 2007 I was promoted to general manager at Ritz-Carlton. Over the past thirteen years, I was able to grow into an area general manager role, and now general manager and vice president overseeing other luxury properties of Marriott International.

I outline the lessons I've learned and practiced, and I will show the ways you, too, can become a mentor and a leader, the importance of furthering your technical competencies, soft skills, and overall knowledge about the business, and the critical aspects of understanding culture and how the world functions.

This book will guide you, help you, and hopefully inspire you to become the best that you can be by working harder and smarter than everyone else. I've learned from and mentored employees at hotels of various sizes and types around the world and have seen that the qualities that make excellent hotel professionals are universal: competency, drive for excellence, integrity, love and passion for what we do, curiosity, hard work and commitment to the goals before us, and authenticity.

An early mentor taught me that a hotel is like the stage of a theater or a movie set, where you perform at your absolute best but where the star of the show is the guest. Your part, together with your team and colleagues, is as a supporting actor, ensuring that the customers feel attended to and important, like a princess or a prince.

As a hotelier or as a leader, manager, or someone with responsibilities to others, you are always under the observation of your staff, guests, partners, and senior leadership. You are constantly measured not by what you say but by what you do.

Your colleagues and bosses will recognize your competence and drive to assist and to work harder. They will ensure you get recognized sooner or later. Ultimately, you do the work to improve the overall environment and you assist because a guest expects the best from you and the team. All this will help you learn, become more skilled, and show what being a true leader is all about—even though you might not have the title yet. You will earn your formal leadership titles with improved competency and all the things you do to improve yourself and your team members. But it's important to remember that the biggest recognition you receive is always the smile and gratitude from someone else for what you do.

You will learn throughout this book that you can achieve everything you want and dream of by starting with yourself, working hard and smart, and using every opportunity to learn and grow. Don't wait until someone asks you to do something—demonstrate initiative by taking action on your own. Be aware of your environment at all times, seek out the challenges around you, never be shy to give your support to a colleague, and most importantly, remain modest and do not wait for a "thank you."

It is really all up to you to grasp success and to lead the efforts to achieve greatness.

This book is organized into two parts. In part one, I will tell you my own story as a hotelier, an overview of the history of the hotel business and the concept of hospitality as it shapes our work today, the education and training necessary to master a career in "the people business," and the career path in the hotel industry. It speaks to the needs and goals of new and rising professionals and will serve as reminders and guideposts for executives with years of experience behind them.

Part two addresses the aspirations and skills necessary for anyone in the hotel industry and beyond who wants to develop as a leader and an executive to achieve sustainable success in the people business. It speaks to anyone who wants to become a role model and actively mentor others. The eight principles I introduce will help anyone who wants to further their proficiency in all aspects of management, people skills, personal development, and leadership qualities. The concepts can be applied and refined on a daily basis and throughout your career as you seek excellence every day and pursue your professional dreams.

My journey is and continues to be filled with incredible memories made by people, from people, through people. Just like my late father was to me, I want this book and my continued professional life to serve as a role model to all aspiring young and talented hoteliers, existing hoteliers, and to all seasoned and up-and-coming professionals who are seeking to create their own mastery and success in work and life.

PART ONE

CHARTING A PATH FOR SUCCESS IN THE HOSPITALITY AND PEOPLE BUSINESS

CHAPTER ONE
MY PERSONAL STORY:
A JOURNEY OF A LIFETIME

I don't know what your destiny will be, but one thing I do know: the only ones among you who will be really happy are those who have sought and found how to serve.
—*Albert Schweitzer*

I was raised in Baden, a small city in Switzerland. In my home country, there are four national languages: French, German, Italian, and Romansh. From an early age, students learn a second Swiss language, as well as English. Switzerland has always been a tourist country, and many English-speaking guests travel frequently to the heart of Europe. My upbringing is full of wonderful memories of love and warmth. I shared the playgrounds with many other children and played loads of games. Our family apartment was in an ideal location, being both next to the forest and close to the city center, so we could run through the woods or look in the shops—the best of two very different worlds, so to speak, all in one place.

Early on I had my first encounter with a hotel when our neighbors built a smaller property with a large restaurant in our neighborhood. I enjoyed seeing this wonderful building go up, playing around it, and then, eventually, playing inside the hotel with the children of the hotel operator.

EARLY PASSIONS

I had my first experience staying at a hotel was when I was ten—we went to a small family resort in the Swiss mountains. It was a completely new adventure for me. I remember how my parents were happy to be in a place where they could simply relax and enjoy—they didn't have to worry about making breakfast, lunch, or dinner, not to mention cleaning. Both of them worked extremely hard, which allowed us to have our first winter vacation together. But what really stuck with me was our introduction to the general manager and his wife, who together managed this smaller hotel. Both were elegantly dressed, and I particularly remember as if it were today his dark-blue jacket with gold buttons. I was so transfixed by those buttons I even counted them. But what was even more special about both of them was their warm and reassuring presence. They were extremely friendly and engaging. I remember my father saying how they were typical hoteliers. His comment intrigued me.

Throughout our stay, the general manager couple seemed to be at the right place at the right time, like magic. We saw one of them when we had breakfast and when we left the hotel for skiing or came back after a long day outside. They always greeted us with a kind word, a suggestion for a fun activity or place to visit, or a sweet treat when we were tired and needed a pick-me-up. I often think back to those special moments of that visit. As I measure myself daily on creating experiences for guests, I try to live the legacy of the true hoteliers, particularly this couple who first inspired me to become a hotelier as well.

My parents, as you'll soon learn, were incredible supporters in all I wanted to do, and because of their generous and loving nature, my brother and I had very happy childhoods. They made sure we knew that we had boundaries and rules, but this made me feel safe and well taken care of.

My late father, who had a loving family but a tough upbringing just before the Second World War, was the eldest son of twelve children. He served proudly in the Swiss Army and protected the border after the Korean War, mostly stationed in Panmunjom. He traveled extensively for his jobs, and he inspired me with his stories from those journeys. It was not easy then to fly from Switzerland to South Korea, Japan, Mexico, and the United States. I remember playing the drums with the chopsticks he had brought back from South Korea. Through him, his experiences, and my curiosity, I knew from an early age that I wanted to travel the world like him, to see people who were different from me, to eat new foods, hear various types of music, see tropical islands and coconut trees, explore the big cities—I wanted to be a global citizen.

My parents encouraged me to participate in sports from a young age. I won my first gold medal when I was only six years old in track and field. I was given the emotional support to push my limits in what I really loved doing. My brother and I trained hard several days a week and we enjoyed the journey throughout.

I discovered another passion, too, playing the trumpet, which took center stage during my earlier years. This instrument was for me like love at first sound. Louis Armstrong was my idol. I dedicated hours to improving my skills, and I learned to create a personal sound focusing on emotions and understanding the music. Onstage, I could feel the audience, which gave me even more inspiration and drive to perfect this craft. I loved the interaction and aimed to become the best at it.

I spent countless hours practicing my trumpet, which was critical to my success at becoming one of the best trumpet players in the country at that time. I had my first taste of leadership when I was the assistant conductor of a youth orchestra in my city, one of the biggest in the country, with more than 120 dedicated musicians. It was an incredible honor and pleasure to conduct this orchestra on several occasions, and it opened up a new world to me. This early lesson in leadership still helps me with my leadership approach today, because I always try to feel the emotions of those around me, closely listen to their words, and guide the people working with me to achieve the perfect melody, bringing all senses to life.

I played in the Swiss Military Band and for the National Youth Brass Band of Switzerland—we even won the world championship! Hard work pays off, and that was the valuable lesson behind the interests I pursued.

My first paying job, apart from some trumpet performances, was when I was fourteen, distributing newspapers in the neighborhood. During my summer holiday, I got up at 4:00 a.m., took my bicycle and started my morning tour of one hour and thirty minutes. When I was nineteen, I moved to San Francisco, where I studied music for more than a year. This helped me with my English, and I learned how to live independently from my family. I also had the opportunity to play in an orchestra in Southern France, which was a great experience. Being able to perform in front of different people every night was rewarding, but I realized that my real dream was to be in direct contact with people.

Based on my early childhood passion and desire for travel and the wonder of hotels, I knew that my future was in hospitality. I left my pursuit of professional music, did my compulsory service in the Swiss Army, and began my journey of service in the industry of my dreams—hospitality.

AN EARLY TASTE FOR THE BUSINESS

As is traditional for many young people in Switzerland, at the age of sixteen I started a professional apprenticeship. I attended class one and a half days a week and spent the rest of my weekdays working for a company. In doing so, I followed in the footsteps of my grandfather, my father, and my brother, who all had early exposure to business.

An apprenticeship allows a young professional to look into various aspects of working in a company. It gave me my first taste of how business functions, and I was able to apply what I learned in my classes immediately in that organization. This apprenticeship took three years. It was a wonderful experience, during which I grew every day. I learned about accounting, sales, and other administrative departments. I was grateful for the opportunity, and I am still in touch with my boss from those years, a wonderful businessperson and owner of that company and someone I looked up to and still admire today.

My hotel career began at the age of twenty-one in a local hotel in Wettingen, a neighboring city to my hometown. I worked at the door, the front desk, and in the restaurant as a server. My father advised me to work in as many parts of the hotel as possible to get a feel for the business and to serve others.

Both of these early experiences opened my eyes to the importance of learning on the job to better serve customers. But it was embarrassing for me on occasions when I was unable to respond to guests in a professional way because I didn't yet know everything about the job. I stumbled in my responses and had to ask for help more than once from my superiors. It became clear to me that training, guidance, and an initiation to the company and brand were absolutely critical to do a job well and to represent the organization with pride and competency.

Of course, as a young professional (and even as a seasoned one), making mistakes is part of the job. Mistakes help you learn, and their by-product is growth and greater insight. With the right attention and support from leadership, you will not only become more solid in your job but will also strengthen your personality and build your confidence to move forward. Even in those early years, I already felt the need for employees to go through an "initiation stage," or as it's called today, an "orientation," prior to starting a job. Every employee needs to receive the right attention and understanding about their company and what it stands for in order to truly become and be part of the team and the brand.

Those fumbles were the inspiration for my obsession with orientation programs for newly selected employees and my belief in a buddy system for trainees, where they can work closely with an experienced team member until they get to know the basics and feel comfortable enough to approach guests on their own.

Before I began my journey, I learned from experienced hoteliers that joining a highly regarded hotel school would assist me with building my career and preparing for a future management role. My dream was to attend the most renowned hotel school in the world, École Hôtelière de Lausanne. The "EHL" was, and still is, famous in all hotelier circles. But having been raised in the German-speaking part of Switzerland, I knew I had to fine-tune my French in order to be admitted. I had taken French in high school, but I was not fluent enough for university-level work. So at the age of twenty-two, I moved to Lausanne to work at the front desk of a smaller local hotel. It gave me the chance to work, save money, and practice my French while experiencing an international hotel environment in a beautiful place alongside Lake Geneva (also known as Lac Leman). It was a great opportunity to engage with guests from all over the world and to learn the trade from my boss. He set high standards, and his drive and commitment to guest satisfaction inspired me to work both harder and smarter.

Professionally, I learned about true mentorship from my general manager. He was a graduate from Lausanne and showed genuine interest in my development. He recognized my talent and willingness to work hard to achieve my goals. He exposed me to different areas of his hotel, such as Food and Beverage and Stewarding, Sales and Marketing, and the role of working the overnight shift to take care of the hotel. It felt great to have someone who was supportive of my growth and who gently pushed me to develop more skills. He helped me discover my strengths and become aware of some of my weaknesses, too. One lesson that I carry with me from his leadership style is to focus on the particular talent of every employee and nurture it to help them achieve their full potential.

I very much enjoyed what I was doing during this period because I really loved the jobs and the environment, and I had no problem motivating myself to work harder. The key to my success and anyone's success is to have the right mentor who believes in you and can spark that further fire through inspiration, showing trust, and genuine care.

This first mentor, M. Dupart, allowed me to make mistakes but asked me constantly about what I was learning. He was there when I needed him, and he was gracious enough to say "Merci beaucoup," or "Great job, Iwan." This constant feedback was absolutely crucial to my growth. He was not shy about taking me to the side and giving me advice or explaining when he observed or heard something that I should have done better or differently. I learned that having a caring boss motivated me to do more, to go above and beyond, and it further increased my drive and desire to bring better results for all involved and make the general manager proud.

I knew I had to work hard to pass the entry exam at EHL, and two years later, with my French at a reasonable level of fluency, I was allowed to start my studies. (Note: Today the school offers classes in English.)

MY YEARS AT ÉCOLE HÔTELIÈRE DE LAUSANNE

École Hôtelière de Lausanne is the oldest hotel school in the world and is known for combining theory with practical work and for its alumni of "Anciens" around the world. The program included alternating weeks in a classroom setting, listening to lectures and presentations, with the other week focusing on practical work, either in the kitchen cooking for all the students or working in housekeeping, at the front desk, or in the bar, depending on your year of study.

As a student, you learn the trade from the ground up. After every semester you are required to do a traineeship in that area, which gives each student further exposure. At the time, the school had only about one hundred students per semester, though this number has increased exponentially since, offering both a full bachelor's degree as well as graduate degrees in hospitality. And of course, other schools in Switzerland and around the world now have similar models, with proven track records of success for their students.

I believe that the school you attend is not the most important thing. If you're true to yourself and you have a passion for learning and a vision for where you want your career to go, you will succeed. With a global workforce, students in your class may be able to share their knowledge and have meaningful interactions with one another. Hopefully, the teachers encourage this, because certainly not all have had the opportunity to have been in South Africa, or China, or Dubai, and so forth, or have been exposed to the newest standards in the industry.

That said, it is absolutely possible to achieve greatness without attending a specialized hotel school. Through mentorship, passion, hard work, and growing from within, many professionals have risen through apprenticeships (culinary, service, administration, etc.) and/or have learned the trade from humble beginnings, without any degree, making their way up to top positions and even leading companies today. So while a solid school can help you, in the end success is about drive and hard work, curiosity, mentorship, learning opportunities, and being part of a company where you can achieve your fullest potential.

For me, the years I spent in Lausanne shaped my professional outlook and gave me more confidence, but they also taught me to remain humble because I realized how much there was to learn. I was lucky to be part of a select few who got to attend this amazing school, and I'm extremely grateful to my parents for allowing me to learn from one of the best. That said, I understood my responsibility as a young professional to represent Lausanne at its finest. People expect the best, and you have to deliver on that every single day.

Once I had my diploma from Lausanne, and a wonderful additional two years as the #2 back at the small hotel where I'd first trained, I felt ready to go out into the hotel world and make a name for myself. I had researched the best hotel companies to join and the most prestigious locations. And if for any reason I could not join the best, I looked into which would be the next in the ranking, which would later allow me to join the best one.

The journey from Lausanne to the United States and the best hotel company in the world was not that smooth, however. I determined that New York City was the place to be: it was the city of dreams. Like Frank Sinatra's famous song, "If I can make it there, I'll make it anywhere…" I was definitely driven to it. I sent out my résumé and obtained interviews with several prestigious hotel companies.

FINDING A PLACE TO BELONG: THE MAKING OF A CAREER

I prepared hard for all the interviews. I learned to be reserved but firm in my desire to join the hotel, and I outlined all my past experiences. I informed the interviewers of my desired dream job, with timeframes, and told them the path I intended to take to get there. Every director of human resources knew exactly why I was interested in the job and what I wanted to become and by when. It was also important for me to learn from them what they would do for their employees and whether the hotels were willing to employ an ambitious yet grounded young hotelier.

Unfortunately, my experiences in four out of the five hotels where I interviewed were disappointing.

Why? Because from the moment I walked into each one of these four hotels, I did not feel welcomed. I did not get the smile and attention I expected; nor did I experience a sense of hospitality and belonging at their heart. Even though I had a diploma from the best hotel school in the world, the doors did not just open. I will not share the hotels' names here, but the disappointing first impressions came from iconic, landmark New York hotels. At one, I went to the front desk to ask where I was supposed to go, and the people who greeted me were rude, not engaging, and made me feel uncomfortable. Instead of showing genuine care and interest in my appointment that day, one particular employee instead told me that I could not come in through the front of the hotel. I remember his words clearly: "You need to leave through the same door you came in, turn to your left, and then to the left again, and then you will see a door for the employee entrance. That's where you need to go."

As you probably can imagine, I was pretty disappointed and did not feel valued as a potential employee. I had never expected this treatment, but it opened my eyes about this company, and others as well. I asked myself many questions about "why." I did not feel that there was an acceptable corporate culture that genuinely engaged their employees or focused on their well-being. The interview was disappointing as well; I could not feel any warmth, nor any genuine interest in really understanding who I was and why or how I could contribute to that organization. Needless to say, I did not end up working there.

This was an important first lesson for me as a future employer and manager. What I could not understand and still do not comprehend is why I, and probably other candidates, were not treated with more consideration. I was invited by the general manager to come for an interview, so why were they not more welcoming? But as with everything, you learn from the experience. Those early interviews were an eye-opener for me on how I would handle the whole experience differently when I became a manager. I asked myself a lot of questions and went through an important journey, learning how critical it is to treat employees with respect and dignity. The experience from that front desk manager made me understand that our business requires people with heart, passion, compassion, and the right attitude to represent the organization and brand at all times.

After a few more disappointing experiences, I received a message from a school friend to come and join her at "one of the best" hotel brands in the Washington, DC, area. Wow, I thought. I hadn't considered expanding my reach to Washington, DC. But I was intrigued and grateful for this message. I started communicating with the hotel and brand that had set new standards in the luxury hospitality industry and scheduled some meetings.

I took the four-hour train ride from New York, and as soon as I arrived for my interview at the Ritz-Carlton, I could immediately see and feel why this company's reputation was so deserved. When I arrived at the front door, I was greeted warmly and then, at the front desk, I was welcomed with "Wonderful to meet you, Iwan! We've been expecting you. How are you? Would you like to follow me?" Wow! It made such an incredible first impression that my heart started to pound with excitement. I felt welcome and a sense of true belonging. Everyone was friendly, no matter who I encountered, and how junior or senior. Throughout my entire interview experience, they treated me with respect. They genuinely cared about me and my interest in joining their organization.

Without hesitation, I accepted their offer to start as a housekeeping manager. Yes, I went from the #2 position at a small boutique hotel after graduating from hotel school to being a housekeeping manager, but I knew this was an opportunity to work for an amazing company that I could learn so much from. I saw how special the corporate culture was from all the employees I'd met, and it already had a profoundly positive impact on me.

I went from a good salary to earning a basic wage, but again, I knew the hit to my income was temporary and would be an amazing trade-off and investment in my growth, strengthening my competencies at the highest level. I was very grateful to learn from all the employees in housekeeping and the rooms division as these wonderful professionals helped me to succeed!

Early on, I could see that the company did business differently. Everyone was committed to creating excellence throughout the hotel and the entire organization, including top executives, particularly the cofounder and president of the company, Mr. Horst Schulze, and throughout all the ranks and positions. The Ritz-Carlton took excellence even further by adapting a total quality management approach in their processes, looking at key metrics, determining the state of the hotel from the viewpoint of their guests, as well as the employees. The organization was one of the first in the hospitality industry to incorporate a particular quality approach into everyone's job, as part of the overall company culture to create excellence, every single day and with every single guest.

I showed up each day with an eagerness to make a difference. My innate sense of curiosity, together with supportive leaders and team members, helped me to learn quickly and allowed me to move up the ranks. I was lucky again to have great mentors, some of whom are now high-level executives in the luxury hotel industry. The person in charge of the rooms division at that time—the one who offered me my first job—became not only a very good friend but a critical mentor, who expected the best from me every day but was never shy to give constructive feedback, setting the bar high for my success.

As a young leader, I focused on inspiring my team members through establishing a work environment based on the philosophy of the company, making sure that everyone was valued, and by continually improving the overall business environment with the employees to create further opportunities for all. We saw great results, and with the support from my employees and immediate managers, I continued to grow by taking specific courses offered by the human resources department, then transferred to other departments to cross-train.

I remained in the United States for several years. Step by step, position by position, I became an executive myself, moving to Dubai to lead the food and beverage (F&B) division of the company's first hotel in the Middle East. Helping to open this important property was a milestone I will never forget. It was a culmination of efforts that proved to me that serving others not only allows you to touch their hearts and bring a smile into their faces, but it also creates the foundation to become a true leader who inspires others to follow you. I learned to work hard, growing by doing, asking questions, and by finding ways to achieve the desired goals.

During this same period, the company went through a phase of incredible growth. They expanded from about thirty hotels to now more than one hundred around the world. Once I achieved my first executive position, my desire to further travel, grow, and experience the world and to contribute to the growth of others in the most beautiful profession—hotelier—only increased.

During the next few years, I was able to continue my journey through the world with assignments in Germany, Egypt, Qatar, then Singapore, followed by my first assignment in China, in the incredible city of Shanghai.

I have lived and worked in thirteen countries and on four continents. My flexibility to move and travel around the world allowed me to continue my learning from various cultures and to strengthen and apply my expertise in different ways, touching the hearts and minds of employees and guests from all walks of life. I became a more global thinker, and all these experiences made me the professional I am today.

Everywhere I worked, I felt as if every day was new, and it allowed me to learn and stay hungry for new adventures. I learned to stay curious, as this is something that many people and so-called experienced hoteliers seem to lose. This concept is sometimes called "beginner's mind," and I invite you to embrace this practice throughout your personal and professional journey.

I always ask a lot of questions when I'm in a new city or a new country, and then I listen. As a hotelier, you need to embrace differences and new environments. It is up to you to learn and show genuine interest in new opportunities.

In my current role as a general manager, I manage a luxury hotel with about five hundred employees in China. In addition, as a regional vice president (Marriott International, Luxury), I oversee six other hotels in the region. As the leader, I am currently in charge of the overall smooth running of the operations. I support the general managers and their teams, helping them to exceed expectations of all the stakeholders, to eventually achieve financial success.

I'm fortunate to work with like-minded coworkers and leaders who come to work every single day to create excellence, to get one step closer to fulfilling their own professional aspirations. As a VP of multiple hotels, I work closely with those general managers and teams to strengthen their business acumen. I support and guide them where they need help and assist them in keeping great relationships with the various owners of those properties. I give them critical advice on business, strategies, and leadership, and together with other senior leaders, including my immediate boss and longtime mentor, I communicate with them often to ensure they feel comfortable with expectations that have been set and assist their teams in their ongoing efforts to excel.

All my experiences from the past shaped my skills of today, allowing me to excel in my job functions as a general manager and VP and as a leader. I want you to be aware that you create your own opportunities by doing a task and becoming a master at it, bringing your expertise with you as you move to the next position or a higher level through a promotion. A great way to imagine and prepare yourself for your next position is to "put on the hat" of your next desired role and the job responsibilities that come with it. Visualizing, learning, and thinking from your desired next job will allow you to be more focused on your growth. It will help you create a clear approach of how to structure every single day. I want you to be in charge of your own destiny and not delay one day in building your career.

Part of that ownership of your career is to truly understand what makes you successful, what makes you a great hotelier—which we'll turn to now.

CHAPTER TWO
THE HISTORY OF THE HOTEL BUSINESS:
A RICH HERITAGE

The customer is never wrong.
—César Ritz, Hotelier of Kings and King of Hoteliers

As leaders in the hospitality business, it's important to understand the rich heritage of our industry, how it began, and where we will be going as we move into the future.

Before I go more deeply into the history of what I believe is the most beautiful profession in the world, allow me to explain the word "hotel." The origin of the word "hotel" in English, where the generic meaning was used to indicate "lodging," has its root in the Medieval Latin word "hospitalis," which translated means "hospitable." It comes from the Latin words "hospes" and "hostis," which translate into "host," to be friendly with guests, to welcome others with care and warmth.

Hospitality is the art of entertaining and receiving guests. In other words, you, as a host, offer hospitality to others. As a hotelier and host, you have the power to create lifelong memories for your guests, and you ensure this through your professionalism, focus, and heart-warming service to others. We all have the great opportunity to bring this philosophy of "hospitalis" to life by engaging friends and guests and anyone we encounter. A true hotelier makes others feel welcome and shows genuine care with an approach that "touches hearts" through concern for people's well-being.

The history of the hotel business goes back a long way and is intimately connected with civilization as it evolved. It has even been theorized that the famous Lascaux caves, where the very first cave drawings have been found, are considered to be the first shelter where accommodation of people from a different tribe can be proven.[1] The exact date of the caves is unclear, but they are said to be from as far back as 38,000 to 15,000 BCE.

The international hotel consultant and educator Jacques Levy-Bonvin wrote in his overview of the business, "Hotels: A Brief History,"[2] that facilities offering hospitality for guests have been recorded since early biblical times. Various civilizations created areas and facilities for travelers to rest, like the Greeks, who developed thermal baths, and later the Romans, who provided accommodation for travelers on official government business.

As a Swiss, I learned during my early school days that the Romans were instrumental in the development of thermal baths in Europe, in particular in the city of my birth, Baden (Canton of Aargau). Baden became known for having the highest level of minerals in the water in the area. The warm mineral waters were thought to be healing, and thus became a desired Roman destination. The word "spa" actually comes from the Latin phrase "Salus per aquam," which means "health through water." Baden has remained a tourist destination for the past two thousand years, and you can still view Roman coins and artifacts in the local museum. There are other great spa destinations in Europe and around the world, each of them with their own unique history.

In the early 700s, the first ryokans (inns) opened in Japan. There are many still in operation today, often located in areas of natural beauty.

As trade opened up along the Silk Road, resting places for caravans and guesthouses opened up.

In the Middle Ages, monasteries and abbeys offered travelers a place to rest, and these early religious hoteliers built hospices and simple stopping places for people traveling when they went on pilgrimages. Traveling at that time was a hazardous journey, and more and more inns for merchants appeared in Europe during this period.

The 1600s were an interval of huge growth for inns in England and France. These inns played a vital role in the evolving and prospering economic, social, and political life, and the innkeepers became some of the influential members of the society. One of the famous places at that time in the late-sixteenth century is still one of the top luxury hotels in Switzerland: the L'Auberge, or as it is called now, L'Hotel des Trois Rois in Basel. It was founded in 1681 as an inn and became a grand hotel in 1844, hosting famous guests such as Napoléon Bonaparte, Empress Michiko of Japan, Duke Ellington, Charles Dickens, and Pablo Picasso. A grand hotel is defined as a large luxurious hotel with a traditional architectural style. These grand hotels began to flourish in the late 1800s in Europe and North America. The first establishment to call itself a hotel was the Grand Hotel in London, which opened in 1774.

The industrial revolution, with steamships, trains, and the rise of commerce, meant more travel for everyone. In the United States, the first hotel built specifically for that use was opened in 1794: the seventy-room City Hotel on Broadway in New York City. US hospitality evolved through the first luxury hotel built in any city center: the Tremont House in Boston, which opened in 1829 (and closed toward the end of the century). It hosted such notable guests as Davy Crockett and Charles Dickens. The special offerings at that time included inside toilets, locks on the doors, and a dining menu.

Throughout America, hotels were built along the rail lines. Luxury hotels opened in the mountains as an escape from the heat in the summer, including places such as the Mount Washington Hotel in New Hampshire and the Grand Hotel on Mackinac Island, Michigan, and in warmer climates as an escape from the cold in the winter, like the Palm Beach Inn, later known as the Breakers, in Palm Beach, Florida.

The evolution of the hotel business in Europe continued with the transformation of the Palace in Venice, Italy, in 1822, which became Le Danieli. In Switzerland, the iconic hotel L'Hôtel des Bergues was built in early 1834 on the shore of the Lake of Geneva. This hotel still exists today. Two more iconic hotels were built in Switzerland during the same period, L'Hotel des Trois Couronnes in Vevey and the Baur au Lac in Zurich. In 1863, the first international hotel in modern Chinese history, The Astor Hotel, opened in the Tianjin, China. It was built in the former

British concessional district and still exists today. Gradually, hotel infrastructure became more sophisticated. In 1898, César Ritz, from the Valais in Switzerland, who became, to quote the famous phrase of King Edward VII, the "king of hoteliers and hotelier to kings," opened the Ritz in Paris, which bears his famous name.

Tourism opened in the mountain regions in Europe, particularly in Switzerland, in fantastic ski resorts like Saint Moritz, where the Swiss hotel pioneer Caspar Badrutt opened the famous Badrutt's Palace in 1896. In 1913 the Gstaad Palace launched its operations. It is one of the last independently owned iconic luxury hotels in Switzerland, owned and operated by the Scherz family for three generations, a pioneer in the luxury hotel business. Royalties and celebrities have made the Gstaad Palace their home for now more than a century. Back in New York, the Roosevelt Hotel opened in 1924 and was the first hotel to incorporate storefronts instead of lounges in its sidewalk facades, as it was against the law to have any bars due to Prohibition. In 1927, the Statler Hotel in Boston opened its doors (now called the Boston Park Plaza). The hotelier E. M. Statler built this hotel as a prototype of the grand American hotel, calling it the "city within a city," as it was adjacent to an office building.

In the 1950s, the hotel industry experienced a second boom due to many airline companies developing their own properties in key locations around the world. Many big and well-known hotel companies had tremendous growth during these times, pioneering modern hospitality the way we know it today. The tourism sector in the Mediterranean started to flourish mostly in the 1960s, with developments in Spain and Greece, followed by Portugal. People loved to be exposed to more exotic locations to enjoy the sun and were eager to relax and enjoy the warmth. Disneyland opened just south of Los Angeles in 1955, and Disney World opened in Orlando, Florida, in 1971. Theme resorts became another reason to travel.

The actual "boom" for business travelers started in the seventies, with the construction of business hotels. Travel for business became easier with new airlines and airports and companies extending their global reach.

The Middle East started to attract business travelers due to the discovery of oil in the region. Many hotels were constructed to open this market to the world. I was lucky to be part of the opening of the first true luxury hotel in Dubai in 1997, then in Doha, Qatar, in 2001. This started an incredible boom to attract both travelers on expense accounts and tourists from around the world. Many countries in the Middle East have flourished tremendously over the past decades and have established themselves as important international destinations.

The trend to offer better amenities for guests (bigger rooms, more varieties of food, local activities, etc.) continued with the bigger hotel companies (chain hotels) focusing on matching increased guest wishes. Concierge services became important, not only to offer additional options for guests, but to promote the local attractions and "tailor make" stays for guests.

In China's more recent history, hospitality opened up in the late 1970s, bigger hotel companies entering the market with international amenities to attract foreign customers. The growth of the Chinese hotel industry has increased exponentially since the economic reforms started in 1978, opening its doors to business and tourist travelers. China has several important local hotel chains, including Shanghai Jin Jiang International Hotels Group, which is the largest hotel company in China. In September 2015, Jin Jiang hotels acquired a substantial stake in Keystone Lodging Holdings, which owns Plateno Hotels Group, and various others, creating one of the world's largest hotel groups. The Huazhu Hotels Group owns and operates various local brands and entered an alliance with Accor in 2016. The Shangri-La Hotels and Resorts Group is an important player in Asia, particularly with its many luxury hotels in China. The company was founded in 1971 and is managed out of its headquarters in Hong Kong. Shangri-La Hotels were instrumental in the growth of the sector in Asia and in China, particularly in the luxury segment.

The growth of the travel industry and hotel business was rapid through the 1990s and early 2000s and, except for times of retrenchment, it has continued steadily, particularly in emerging markets like Southeast Asia and India as well as China. An important factor that has made a huge impact are the various technological advances throughout this and many other industries. Today, a hotel is operated and managed somewhat differently from a decade ago. It's important to keep in mind that the human touch and skills of the employees to manage all aspects of a hotel must always be there, because a hotel can't operate without the hands, hearts, and minds of many people, but technological advances have changed the equation. Today, we have to work harder than ever to keep the principle of "hospitalis" at the heart of what we do.

Hotel facilities have become complex constructs, where various parties, including designers, architects, specific F&B specialists, "creators," and many others come together to design venues that meet or exceed the countless expectations of modern travelers. As hoteliers, we need to constantly evolve to ensure that the hotel of the future can achieve the best and highest standards of the more and more sophisticated travelers from around the world, and in particular from emerging markets. For the next generation entering and rising in the hospitality business, the key aspects of operating a hotel successfully will not change. However, Millennials and GenZs in particular will discover ways of utilizing the ever-changing advancements in technology to enhance service and product delivery in numerous and exciting ways. Many hotel companies have already developed designs, layouts, and functionality to adapt to the needs and expectations of the newer generations. Innovations happen continually, and everyone can contribute today to the hotel of tomorrow. In some ways, this "hotel of tomorrow" has already been created by Mr. Jack Ma, the founder of Alibaba, a great entrepreneur and leader. His FlyZoo Hotel in Hangzhou, China, is entirely cashless and operates almost entirely with robots, uses facial recognition doors, and most of the communication happens through the hotel's app.

International hotel companies are catching up fast, particularly with the possibilities to utilize applications for greater ease and efficiency. These new tools allow guests to make reservations, book their in-room dining, communicate with the employees directly, and speak to a more tech-savvy clientele.

China, for example, has evolved from an emerging country to the second most important economy in the world in a short period of time. I was fortunate to see and experience this tremendous evolution; hotels in China today represent the best of the best.

Enormous investments were made in building hotels around the country. Chinese tourists will become the most important travelers in the coming years. The Chinese middle class has grown at a rapid clip and now represents about four hundred million people, and their eagerness to travel the world increases year after year. This offers hoteliers around the world a great opportunity. The new expectations of travelers need to combine excellent infrastructure, top technology, exciting offerings, and most importantly, capable employees who can create long-lasting and special memories for guests.

Having lived and still living in China, I strongly believe that the tremendous growth opportunities for the hotel industry in China and various parts of Asia, as well as the entire African continent, will continue for years to come. It is now up to the companies and leaders to create the next local generation of hoteliers by inspiring talented individuals to achieve greatness every day and in everything they do.

The people in these countries have opened up to the hospitality industry. They are excited to be hosts, to contribute to the growth of the industry. They are ready to welcome guests and extend their hospitality to the world and are dedicated to continuously learning and growing in order to shape their own story about the hotel industry in China. I am thrilled to be part of improving and strengthening this sector by leading by example every day and demonstrating excellence at all times. I am constantly energized by having the daily opportunity to serve and lead by example—to "walk the walk," as the familiar saying goes.

The innovations of the past and today can inspire a new era, which we can't yet imagine. Innovation can be defined as the process of creating value by applying novel solutions to meaningful problems. I personally like this definition as it explains that an innovation is incremental, a step-by-step approach, improving on or making a significant contribution to an existing product, process, or service. Throughout the history of hospitality, many new concepts emerged. I can only mention a few, which I believe are interesting to read about. As a professional in our business, perhaps you can do your own research and add to the list. It's always important and interesting to learn from history and the past. As you are passionate about our industry, I am sure you will have your own creative innovations to add, now or sometime in the future. You shape the hospitality business, and you will grow through new inventions and ideas.[3]

Here are just a few milestones of technology in the hotel industry:

- In 1829, Tremont House in Boston offered indoor toilets, locks on the doors, and bellboys.

- In 1832, Holt Hotel in New York had the first steam-powered elevator.

- In 1870, Palmer House Hotel in Chicago had telephones installed in all rooms and were fire-resistant.

- In 1893, the first hotel school in the world, Ecole Hoteliere de Lausanne, was founded and the Waldorf Astoria in New York was the first hotel to offer room service.

- In 1927, the Statler Hotel in Boston provided the first in-room radios.

- In 1947, the Roosevelt Hotel in New York included television sets in all rooms.
- In 1969, the Westin Hotel Group implemented twenty-four-hour room service.
- In 1983, the Westin Hotel Group was first to offer reservations and checkout using major credit cards.
- In 1993, the digital age began; newly created software allowed hotels to offer online bookings through reservations systems, operations management tools, guest preferences, and loyalty programs.
- In 1994, Hyatt Hotels and Promus Hotel Corporation became the first hotel chains to launch websites on the internet.
- In 2003, hotel Wi-Fi saw a steady increase, as more than six thousand hotels made it available to guests.
- In 2010, Apple released its first iPad, and the first in-room iPad made an appearance at the Plaza in NYC.
- In 2016, Henn-na Hotel, the world's first robot hotel, opened in Japan.
- In 2019, Alibaba's Jack Ma introduced facial-recognition technology as a way to enter the guest rooms of his high-tech hotel in Hangzhou, China.

Additional developments with technology include:
- Experiments with virtual reality as part of the rooms amenities allow guests to order a virtual trip through

room service or any other parts of the hotel (pioneered by Marriott International).

- Smartphone-operated rooms make it possible for guest to control their room remotely through a mobile phone or tablet, allowing them to turn on the TV, browse and order food, and so on. Many hotels already offer those services, but this can be further improved and adapted more generally and globally.

- Artificial Intelligence (AI) is probably the most profound example of how hotel technology is advancing. AI will allow hotels to create more seamless overall experiences, through mapping and identifying guest preferences to create a tailor-made personalized package. This technology creates new and untouched possibilities.

I know that you will further contribute to this list with your innovative spirit, your leadership, your know-how, enthusiasm, and your relentless drive to "create."

CHAPTER THREE
THE EXPERIENCE OF HOSPITALITY:
THE GUEST EXPERIENCE

When you get into a hotel room, you lock the door, and you know there is a secrecy, there is a luxury, there is fantasy. There is comfort. There is reassurance.
—*Diane von Furstenberg*

A hotel is not simply a place where people eat, drink, and rest for the night or a resort where one can get a much-needed vacation. For those of us who work there, it represents a place where it is our privilege to host and serve others—our guests. Regardless of the size of the hotel, the amenities offered, or the location of the property, the service for guests should always feel seamless, professional, and friendly, and I believe it should come with a local flair and feel. Yes, technology is becoming more important—as a necessity and an expectation. But the warmth of the employees and their understanding of how to make people feel welcome are the critical elements that will always be our business. It is up to all of us, and the new generation of professionals coming of age, to keep them alive and well.

When I look at the experience in hospitality, I come back to the origins of hosting. What does that look like and how does it feel, whether I'm serving people within the luxury model, staying at a basic hotel on a road trip, or *visiting* a remote town and staying at a local inn. What does "hospitality" mean to a new generation of travelers? Is there a way to keep the focus on comfort and rest, where the guest leaves with a smile, that remains universal, even if it looks different in our more technology-driven businesses and lives?

Many luxury hotel companies and owners invest a lot of money into the location, the infrastructure, and the overall look and feel of a hotel. While these are important aspects of any hotel, leaders need to be able to match that money spent by going above and beyond guest expectations and create equal value not just in the looks of a property but through professionalism, service, leadership, and the focus on guest engagement.

Hospitality in its truest form is about ensuring that the intangible aspects of serving others receive as much genuine care as the tangible ones. Everyone needs to constantly be thinking about how the customer's experience would be without any furniture, without any artwork on the walls or a beautiful view. How would the guest experience the hotel if it solely relied on the interactions with the staff? That is the ultimate experience of hospitality, because a hotel should not feel like it's a museum that is too beautiful to touch. Tasteful decor, lavish artwork, fabulous design elements, rich carpets, and elaborate chandeliers do not replace the warmth and conscious competence of the employees—the hosts. All this opulence needs to be elevated by knowledgeable, genuinely caring employees who understand the difference between arrogance, elegance or aloofness, and making guests feel special.

I've had many experiences throughout my travels where employees felt that they were more important than the guest, in particular in hotels where the reputation of the hotel is bigger than the actual experience. This attitude has always been a great disappointment to me, for it's not what being in the "people business" is about. Quite the opposite is true. I invite you to remember your own humanity at all times. This will help you connect with the heart of why you began your journey of service. Our business is not about the environment and who can afford to stay there. It is about how guests are made to feel. The entire staff must bring the hotel to life through their unique personalities, competence, and warmth in order to give the guest the best experiences and to create priceless memories.

A hotel, or any establishment in the "people business," should and needs to be a welcoming experience where people know how to engage and take care of guests' needs, where skilled employees go above and beyond to create a unique and unforgettable experience.

Being in the hospitality business is about understanding how to individualize each encounter you have with a guest so that the other person feels naturally enriched.

The people business is the art of dealing, engaging, and communicating with people in a way that warms their hearts, makes them feel good about themselves, and ensures that their experience is one where they can learn and grow with every interaction. You can help create long-lasting memories and give guests a positive and inspiring feeling. After all, when people are away from home, whether it be on a business trip, or as a tourist, they are naturally out of their element and feel vulnerable and out of place. It is our job as hoteliers to make guests feel welcome and comfortable in their temporary home away from home. We have to learn how to give without expectation of receiving, to innately capture others' hearts with our ability to be authentic and empathetic. And the intangible rewards that we receive from our guests, such as bright smiles, warm thank-yous, and genuine compliments, for example, inspire and often energize us. I find these things to be invaluable perks of our jobs. I hope you do too.

What I love about hotels is that this is where the world is united all under one roof, where professionals from all walks of life come together, and employees—professionals in the people business—dedicate themselves to putting smiles on guests' faces. Smiles are gifts that keep on giving, so remember, what you do matters. In our business, we treat everyone with the utmost attention, without any judgment. A hotel is a feel-good environment, where people come first. All people, regardless of their heritage, background, and orientation are to be treated equally yet individually. They should be treasured, welcomed as family.

Why do customers choose to stay in one hotel over another? Clearly, personal preferences, the reason for the visit, budget, and numerous other factors play a critical role. A less expensive hotel option does not mean that it is acceptable for employees to smile less and serve the coffee cold. It does not mean that the hotel rooms can be neglected—not cleaned properly and not maintained fastidiously—and that the general manager and all management do not need to be visible, greeting guests, and instead simply stay in their offices to work on bottom-line issues. No, lower cost, non-luxury status does not invite mediocrity. This is still a service profession, and the practices necessary to demonstrate this must be smoothly executed by all—from the top down and the bottom up—whether you serve at a budget or an elite brand establishment.

Subpar service is never acceptable in the hotel business, nor in any other service industry, because the essence and core of a hotel's mission does not change, regardless of price, location, age of the property, number of received stars, or local classification.

Service and creating unmatched memories is our business model. It is time for everyone to start thinking more constructively and seriously about the essence of our business—about what is important in our industry, what makes a hotel successful, and how that success can be sustained.

Every business leader has a responsibility toward the various pillars of the organization, starting with the employees, then guests, company, ownership, and the community.

Without our employees we have no business, no service, and certainly no heart.

Without connecting to and constructively contributing to our communities, we will undermine a major stakeholder in our success.

Without understanding and meeting the needs and expectations of our owners, we are not meeting our responsibility for sustainable and healthy financial success. The hotel business is a for-profit business, and we are responsible for creating, earning, and sustaining profits for our owners and other stakeholders. Even if you operate your own business, you need to guarantee a certain return. Our collective aim is to ensure that owners, management, and the company are happy with the financial performance of the hotel. Period. Various owners have different financial expectations, and few are happy to have a modest return not to have to reinvest any further liquidity.

CREATING MEMORABLE GUEST EXPERIENCES

A hotel is more than just a room.

Here are some of the areas where it is absolutely vital for any hotel, particularly high-end hotels, to create an exceptional experience and where team members in any type of establishment can have a huge impact on guests.

A memorable guest experience requires every employee in all parts of the hotel to play her or his role like a Swiss watch, with its parts in perfect alignment with one another to function without interruption or failure. Those classic mechanical timepieces have anywhere from 130 pieces to more than 1,700. Professionals craft those elements to create a watch that works for a lifetime and hopefully for generations. Every part is important and is mastered to allow the movement to work perfectly.

Creating a flawless guest experience throughout a hotel requires everyone to play their part in the same seamless and interconnected fashion, creating experiences that hopefully will be remembered for a lifetime.

When I was a member of a junior state championship track team in the five by eighty meters, every team member worked in tandem and with the coach. He understood how to lead by example, inspiring us by establishing clear guidelines, requiring hard work, and individualizing training plans to get the most out of the athlete based on personal and mutual goals. Teamwork was crucial, and knowing our peers well was important to our success. Handing the baton from one to the other at full speed takes focus, training, and trust in one another. It is a team sport. On our team, success and failure were shared equally, even when someone made a mistake, like dropping the baton or overstepping the line when handing it to the next teammate. I learned early on how important it is to work closely with others to achieve joint success. It was my responsibility to train hard to improve my physical strength, speed, and technique as an individual performer while complementing my teammates so we could achieve greatness together.

In a hotel, "relay stations" are *experience points* in various areas. They are where skilled employees guide guests from one area to another in a flawless manner. A customer should never have to ask where to go or how to get somewhere in the hotel. Encounters with guests should always be flawless. At every experience point an employee should take the first step to engage with guests empathetically to welcome and assist them. Think of hoteliers as if they are carrying guests on a soft pillow throughout their stay. The expert hotelier makes the guest feel like they are the most important person in the world, protected and safe. They show they are excited that the guest is staying with them and give the customer an experience where they can delight and surprise them with all the offerings of the hotel.

Relay stations can be critical junctions where the guest needs assistance to continue their journey through the hotel without having to ask for it. In any establishment where they are a customer, guests want to feel taken care of, made to feel special and safe, but even more so in a luxury environment. Robotically assisting with needs is not meaningful. Every time we have an opportunity to encounter and engage a guest, it is an opportunity and the job of people professionals to enchant and create a memory. It is how we, as professionals, engage a guest, greet a guest—with our posture, our verbiage, our ability to read their behavior and utilize it to create a bond of trust—that ensures the customer feels personally attended to, both in the heart and mind. Furthermore, relay stations are in all areas of the hotel, where employees rely on others to create unforgettable experiences for our guests.

Teamwork is critical, and flawless execution from each member of the team is an absolute must to achieve that all-important "WOW" from every customer. Relay stations are the seamless service infrastructure within the hotel, and each "play" by the staff is crucial in ensuring the magic we promise to deliver to every client, every time. Everything I talk about in this book needs to come together each time we encounter a guest. This becomes a moment of truth—and the result of that interaction means either the customer is delighted and happy or somewhat disappointed or not really satisfied, which will hurt the establishment and the brand and potentially future business as well.

I would sum up the various experience zones as:

- Reservations or point of making the reservation
- Arrival areas
- Check-in/Check-out (front-of-the-house experience)
- Guest room, housekeeping, laundry (overall experience in the room area, including cleanliness, quality of facility, materials used: sheets, towels, amenities, etc.)
- General hotel areas (food and beverage, banquets, spa, gym, any public area)

- Departure experience
- Follow-up (post-stay)

Many companies, brands, and individual hotels have their own processes to enchant their guests. These vary, but they should always focus on exceeding guest expectations.

RESERVATIONS

The hotel journey starts during the reservation process, through either the reservations phone call to the hotel, a company's reservations center, or a reservation platform. Many customers nowadays prefer to use an app or a website to book their stay. The app or the online presentation needs to offer a welcoming feeling, one that builds anticipation over how great the guest's stay will be. This will be shown through perfectly chosen verbiage, pictures, easy-to-read and understandable processes, and with a clear outline and message to the guest about what can be expected during the stay. That first contact should be an opportunity to cross-sell other areas of the hotel, for instance spa services or a night of fine dining at the hotel; therefore, the designer of the app or website needs to clearly understand the rules of marketing to achieve sales.

Other guests prefer to speak with a professional when making reservations, not only to ask questions and to get immediate responses and feedback, but also to get the feel of the hotel and to imagine more realistically how a stay can be through that first contact with the hotel and brand. While online reservations can show you pictures of the property, there is nothing like speaking with someone who knows the hotel inside and out for information about the specific hotel.

The guest needs to feel welcomed when they call, and the employee on the phone needs to engage with a smile in order to make the customer feel important and to create a special atmosphere of hospitality and enthusiasm during that process. A guest wants to delve into a world where the employee anticipates their needs and is able to read their wishes and desires.

ARRIVAL EXPERIENCE/FRONT-OF-HOUSE EXPERIENCE POINTS

This is the beginning of the senses journey for our guests on property, where they take in the sights, sounds, smells, taste, and touch of the hotel. As I said earlier, the lobby should not feel like a cathedral or a museum. The arrival experience—the human touch, the competency of the employees—needs to complement and enhance the pleasing decor, beautiful artwork, and even the best view. A cooling glass of cucumber- or strawberry-infused water might be offered for the refreshing taste, or the guest can be checked in from the comfort of a relaxing chair. The scent of eucalyptus or a bouquet of fragrant blooming tropical flowers might make their senses feel transported. A stunning piece of artwork might attract the eye, or a waterfall built into the side of the wall can attract both sight and sound.

It is vital to make the guest feel welcome with a smile and enthusiasm and to make the customer feel completely taken care of through professional and engaging behavior. If possible, an employee should use the guest's name during each interaction, to get the customer's full attention and to create a sense of belonging and familiarity. (Please always be discreet about names and personal information.) This should be accomplished with a professional demeanor, eye contact, and an acceptable distance but with a clear focus on the customer.

The first impression made by the hotel and its staff sets the tone for what is to come. You can win guests or lose them from the first interaction. Every employee must have not only the specific knowledge for their department, but the overall familiarity about any other area of the hotel or establishment so that they can facilitate any requests the guest might have. As people professionals, we must ensure that the information we convey to our guests is clear and complete, and if not, always ask for further clarification on what they need with the most delightful manners. The guest is your shining star, and it is your job as a supporting actor to give the limelight, exposure, and a warm-hearted feeling to your guest.

GENERAL HOTEL AREAS (FRONT OF HOUSE)

The Rooms Division plays a critical role in the smooth running of a hotel. As stated above, it represents the first point of contact. In addition to managing all the rooms, it offers important services, such as the concierge and other revenue-contributing outlets, including the spa, the fitness center, the gift shop, or in some luxury hotels, the club lounge.

Those hotel areas, including all food and beverage (F&B) outlets, create the reputation of the establishment as well as the connection with the local community.

The F&B areas are key to any hotel. Restaurants, bars, and banquet spaces showcase a property to local customers and build the needed bond with the community. Any business needs to be closely associated with the local environment, and the F&B areas, including the spa and the gym, offer a great opportunity to create a close relationship with guests.

I enjoyed my time working in F&B. Performing in this role around the world in various positions has allowed me to learn about local cultures through their food and customs. I've always appreciated exploring the different dishes offered up from our talented chefs. A restaurant comes alive through deliciously authentic food, and excellent service allows us to further elevate this art to the customers. All aspects of creating lasting memories—as highlighted throughout this book—are critical, but each has its own particular aspects that are crucial to achieving sustainable success. F&B requires many additional proficiencies and a thorough understanding of and passion for food and beverage.

Both in-house guests and local patrons will talk about their experiences at your hotel's restaurants through social media and other means. Many customers have become self-appointed experts and know exactly what they want and how they want it, but they still expect to be surprised by seasoned, knowledgeable employees. As a hotelier, you want to ensure that you can entice your hotel guests to dine within the hotel and become a destination for your local customers. Restaurants within hotels need to compete with freestanding restaurants specializing in different offerings, so it is necessary for hotels to create unique spaces and position them in the market as more "independent."

For years, many hotel restaurants did not have good reputations, as their food and decor seemed boring and the design like an extension of the hotel's "look and feel." It became evident that these important spaces needed to be operated and promoted differently. The business of F&B has evolved tremendously, and many restaurants, particularly independent operators, became local destinations. Hotel operators had no other choice than to innovate their spaces and to rethink the various options and offerings to compete in this space.

But now there is no reason why a hotel guest has to go outside to find food and beverage. This is a great challenge in the age of endless options, but it is critical for any business operator to create a desirable environment by focusing on excellence in both product and service. I always believed that every outlet, be it a buffet restaurant, a bar, or a fine-dining establishment, should always be first in its class compared to any other establishment outside the hotel. The key is to build that reputation one guest after another and to consistently surprise and captivate the guests with an array of incredible options.

I was able to refine my people skills every single day by working in F&B, be it at the buffet station serving delicious food for guests or at the front of the house, creating an excellent experience. The guest contact and the opportunity to fine-tune your engagement skills are very much a focus in F&B, and it opened my eyes to better understand and read people. I hope that you can further develop your competencies in this special art, as I believe it will help you with your development as a people professional.

Banquet and catering spaces have various functions, but as the areas are important in size, revenues need to be substantial to support an expected return. Most often, there is a separate team in charge of sales for these spaces (Catering Sales as part of S&M), be it for groups, functions, local events, or in-house guests and company meetings. These particular venues represent great top-line opportunities and can help with the overall revenue in F&B. It is important for anyone wanting to become a director of F&B to have worked in this area, in both sales and then executing on the floor as part of the banquet team. That particular venue can seem boring or dry as far as the actual space is concerned, depending on the design. The great challenge and wonderful opportunity for the hotel and its employees is to bring these areas to life, to create the same memories as everywhere else in the hotel.

I was able to work on many different events in my career and always enjoyed the variety of functions that we held. I learned not only to engage and to create repeat business, but also became a great administrator, learning how to organize and then execute various meetings, events, dinners, functions, almost at the same time. Catering is a crucial element to any hotel operation and requires the right understanding, focus, support, employing the right people at the right time, with the right training to elevate the recognition and the hotel reputation in the market.

Every single employee needs to help make a guest's senses come alive, and the best way to teach that is to keep the focus on continuous "senses tests" throughout the hotel. My senses test consists of taking a thirty-second break to absorb the atmosphere. I look at every corner of the room or area while taking a deep breath to inhale the scent and ambience, see and feel the space, and put myself in the shoes of the guest. All my senses need to be inspired and in balance. It is a test of the "feel good" factor. All employees, and particularly leaders, need to exercise this sense awareness to create a top look, feel, and atmosphere on a consistent basis.

People professionals understand how to create memories, not only with their basic skills but through their ability to construct a complete experience by engaging with guests, enlivening all their senses at all times, and touching hearts and minds. At every level of service and sophistication, guests expect to enter a special world while staying at a hotel or when visiting a restaurant or any leisure area. It is up to everyone in the business to create that particular space where guests will think back to the experience as something unique and memorable. Our professionalism requires us to create those special feelings, to inspire our customers, and to help transform them into something unique, creating memories for life.

I would like to highlight the sales and marketing division (part of the front of house). The sales team members are in charge of overall sales (including catering and relationship-development with customers and key accounts) and work closely together with the revenue team to fine-tune offerings based on needs and opportunities to grow the financial health of the business. The marketing and public relations staff help promote the overall hotel and support all its top-line-producing departments. These team members represent the hotel and all the employees when they go for sales calls or promote the hotel. They are important to any success, and you as a leader or future leader want to embrace their professionalism and support them in their quest to improve the visibility of the hotel and overall revenues. We all need to be "salespeople," as every one of us has the direct or indirect responsibility to improve top-line results consistently.

WHAT HAPPENS BEHIND THE SCENES (HEART OF THE HOUSE)

One of the key elements of any hotel experience is, of course, how the guest appreciates the room, their temporary "new home": the overall decoration, comfort, feel, convenience, and most importantly, the cleanliness. Since that is where the guest spends a great deal of their time, it is where they get the biggest impression of the hotel's brand. Housekeeping, laundry, and all the wonderful employees working in what I call "the heart of the house" create those incredible and long-lasting memories that are absolutely key to any successful experience.

Having worked and dedicated several years in those areas of the hotel, I not only became competent about tools, processes, and organizational matters, but I learned how hard these wonderful people work, and with so much dedication, every single day. You, as a future or current leader, need to embrace them and show your complete appreciation for what they do. I learned how I could support them in their needs to actualize excellence and assist them with creating the purpose behind going the extra mile every day.

It takes not only dedication to produce a clean room but also a well-coordinated team to ensure that all areas are in pristine condition. Because a customer not only expects a clean and fresh room but wants to see that all the hardware—the desks, the lamp, and the TV—is in excellent condition and that everything works flawlessly, that the paint is not marked, and the tiles in the bathroom are not chipped. Engineering plays a crucial role in seeing to the flawlessness of the rooms as well, and these teams are made up of a carpenter, painter, and any other expert who can help make the customer feel like they are walking into a brand-new room every time. The different departments that assume those roles need to feel the full support and commitment of leadership. Your job as a leader is not only to engage but to "win" the employees, as they are the "silent success contributors" who deserve your recognition and support at all times.

The heart of the house employees are perhaps less in the spotlight, and guests do not expect to be overly engaged by a housekeeper, a florist, or an engineer, but they should have the same training as everyone else, so a customer might be positively surprised and extremely happy about any interaction they do have.

Two other key areas of the heart of the house that are vital to any business to create sustainable success are finance and accounting (including purchasing) and human resources (HR), which includes the critical department of training and development. These teams of incredible talents make it possible to achieve success throughout the business, and it is up to you, as a line employee, leader, or executive to understand their importance to the overall hotel operations.

You will not be credible as a businessperson if you cannot have solid business conversations with your director of finance or senior people within the HR function. To become a trusted leader and partner, you will have to further improve and strengthen your business acumen. Every day and in any position, you have financial responsibilities. The more senior you get in your career, the more questions you have to answer. Start developing or deepen your business mindset today, as it will help you to understand the financial impact of your decisions as early and clearly as possible.

Human resources is central to any organization and is focused on managing, supporting, and developing employees. These team members assist every leader in the selection process, create training opportunities, and ensure that overall employee satisfaction remains a top priority through the company. You have to fully embrace human resources. It is absolutely vital for any aspiring leader to be part of creating and living the required value system and to support this very important division.

There is and will be a time where you need to not only understand but effectively lead those areas and integrate them into the entire operation of the hotel or organization. Many of these wonderful employees have demonstrated consistently how critical they are and have shown incredible leadership to become successful general managers or corporate leaders in a wide range of companies.

DEPARTURE EXPERIENCE

I am always amazed at how inconsistent the farewell in any establishment can be. It is an absolutely vital "experience point," which really showcases the sincerity and professionalism of the establishment, the understanding of hospitality by the leadership of the venue, to say "Thank you for choosing us."

Often hoteliers neglect this crucial part of the experience. And I believe that we all have a responsibility to do a much better job. Not being at the right place at the right time to say goodbye and to thank the guest for their patronage is a clear failure, regardless of brand, number of stars, or venue. I feel a bit empty when I get up or leave a property without anyone to wish me a good day or to say "Thank you for coming." It feels uncomfortable and clearly expresses to me that we love your money, but sorry, I am too busy to say thank you and I don't care if you choose another establishment the next time around. This type of attitude and lack of attention at the exit point leaves the doors wide open for the competition.

FOLLOW-UP—A POST-STAY GOODBYE IS NOT THE END

A true experience ends with a professional follow-up about the stay or the time spent in one of the other areas of the hotel. It is important to take this part seriously, as feedback is critical. What's even more impactful is the nice message to thank the client sincerely and personally. Many hoteliers again have room for improvement when they follow up with the guest. It is not acceptable to send a general questionnaire asking for client feedback without preceding it with a warm note of gratitude. Building and strengthening customer relationships is the aim of every professional, and that important last step is vital.

It is wonderful to receive a personal email or a note through WeChat or other messenger service. A genuine "thank you" and "it was a phenomenal pleasure to host you" does not cost anything, but it goes a long way. You have an opportunity to bring back those recent hotel memories with a nice and kind personalized message, and if the guest did not have a good experience, then hopefully they will let you know. Never forget that your customer wants you to be successful and hopes that their message back to the hotel will help to create a better bond on a more personalized level with the customer.

If a guest replies or communicates with you directly or by any other means, then please be proactive. Have a great process in place, not just to reply to the guest, but to take any comments or feedback seriously in order to make the recommended improvements. We should all welcome customer feedback and be happy to receive various comments—positive or negative—because we only get better when we look closely at this information. Let's receive this input as a gift in a professional and appreciative way. That will surely further enhance the product or service we offer, thereby allowing us to earn and create more guests for life.

CHAPTER FOUR
THE ROLE OF HOTELIER:
BEING A TRUE HOST

I've learned that people will forget what you said, people will forget what you did, but people will never forget how you made them feel.
—*Maya Angelou*

Most of us probably learned to be a host as we were growing up. At home, we saw the preparation it took to welcome in family, friends, and guests—the shopping, the cleaning, the cooking, the baking—before your parents were able to greet their guests for special dinners, holidays, and parties. Yes, the preparation may have been stressful for your parents. But once the party was in full swing, you could tell every minute was worth it to them. They loved seeing their guests take second helpings of the food they had so carefully prepared. They laughed with their guests and enjoyed how everyone looked so comfortable in the rooms they had cleaned and how happy everyone was at being together.

Now that you're grown, you likely entertain at your own place, and you want to leave a fantastic impression of your abilities as a host. You prepare the house for your special guests by cleaning, especially the kitchen and the bathroom, as everyone tends to gather in the kitchen whether you want them there or not. Your bathroom should be a clean and welcoming place for your guests. (My father used to say the bathroom is the business card of a hotel, restaurant, or the home of any host.)

You prepare a menu, then buy and cook the food, and make it look appetizing on pretty platters and plates, with accompanying wine or beverages at the ready. You decorate your place with flowers, tablecloths, candles, and picture frames. You pick out a nice outfit to impress. As a host, you greet your guests at the front door, lead them into your house explaining where to place their coats and bags, and you introduce them to everyone. As part of a memorable welcome, you will seat your guests and serve them something to drink and, perhaps, some cheese and crackers.

To be a good host starts with you. You are the one in charge. You are the one to show and lead the way, and you are the one who creates those wonderful memories. You don't want your guests to leave with a bad impression or a bad aftertaste, right? If your guest is spending the night, you don't want them remembering that the room was half-cleaned, the pillow was hard, the bathroom was dirty, and you'd run out of coffee for breakfast the next day. I'm not sure your guests would want to stay at your house again if that were the case. Again, you always want to shine and put your best foot forward. Where better than to practice this hospitality—this etiquette—than at home?

Taking care of your family and friends when they visit is not that different from what we do as hoteliers, and on top of that, we get paid for it. That's an added bonus for sure, don't you think? We get to earn our living enhancing the lives of those who visit us—and those people are our very special guests. This is indeed an honor. True hoteliers are here for others. They bring sunshine to people's hearts, create those incredible and unforgettable moments, and ensure that guests leave with a desire to come back. Repeat business in our industry is the highest compliment—this equates to a happy and satisfied customer, one who returns again (and again). These same guests also tell their friends, family, and business associates about the wonderful stay they had while at one of our hotels, served by us.

As a host, you do not want to have your guests unhappy or disappointed in any way by the food or the ambience, or perhaps—even worse—for them to tell others that the food was not good or that they did not feel comfortable during the visit. Right? Well, it's the same in the hotel business. First and foremost, we are in the people business, which is about making others feel good. This is absolutely critical to understand. It is not about you —it is about your guests first.

The most beautiful job is being a host, because it's always about serving others. It means that as a hotelier you need to show that people are the most important. I hope this first lesson is clear. If you have doubts or are not sure what I mean, please ask your parents or your grandparents. That's what they have done and continually try to do for you and your family, to show how much they care for you and want to ensure that you feel good. Just open your eyes and ears and you will understand the importance of taking care of others and making them feel good about themselves. My favorite quote by Maya Angelou, at the start of the chapter, sums it up best: "I've learned that people will forget what you said, people will forget what you did, but people will never forget how you made them feel."

So now let us broaden the definition from host to hotelier.

FROM HOST TO HOTELIER: A PROFESSIONAL

The true meaning of hotelier, as stated in various dictionaries, is a "proprietor or manager of a hotel." Its origins are from the French word *hôtelier*, "hotelkeeper," and from the Old French *ostelier, ostelier*. The true essence of a hotelier is first and foremost to be the host, a professional in the people business, someone who can receive and take care of people—guests—through offering unmatched products and services to create unforgettable experiences.

To be a hotelier not only represents the best profession in the world, but it is a synonym for sophistication. A true hotelier is a connoisseur of *savoir-faire* and *savoir-vivre*—translated to English as "know-how" and the ability to "live elegantly"—a professional who is comfortable in any situation and communicates with ease. A true hotelier is also driven by curiosity to constantly learn and improve knowledge about all areas of life.

A hotelier understands all aspects of the business, is a professional in their approach toward all stakeholders, sets the highest standards at all times, and engages everyone—guests, employees, and those in the community—with the utmost respect. A hotelier, and any top professional in the people business, leaves a positive impact, and most importantly, focuses on touching the hearts and minds of others.

It's fascinating for me to see how many people in the business call themselves "hotelier" without having ever been sincerely involved in creating true excellence; they believe that a hotel can be managed from an office, by focusing only on financial results. But it is my belief, and one that I am convinced contributes to my success, that a true hotelier is visible, demonstrating excellence through engaging and inspiring employees and assisting where needed to focus on the best outcome for both the guests and employees. "Never lose a guest" is a critical slogan that needs to be instilled as a top priority for every hotelier. One's personal involvement in achieving this desired outcome isn't met by pushing employees to reach greater heights. It is the outcome of a company's core values, leadership, technical and emotional competence, and inspired and motivated team members who will do whatever it takes to consistently create greatness for all stakeholders.

FOUR CHARACTERISTICS OF THE HOTELIER'S HEART AND MIND

There are four characteristics that demonstrate the heart and mind of the consummate hotelier.

1. ALWAYS BE A STEP AHEAD (PROACTIVE MINDSET):

A true hotelier is a top professional who understands the importance of "looking ahead" and making appropriate decisions. People professionals anticipate not only business but also the needs and wishes of guests before they become a request or a demand, and furthermore, they think about how their employees feel, think, and act. Our profession is learning and executing based on possible next steps by customers to create that sense of being taken care of and always looking for that opportunity to create a memory moment (MM). Again, a true hotelier needs to strengthen their ability to look one step ahead of anything that might occur within their hotel by engaging patrons and employees in a way to create the next moment for them, or understanding how they might act in a specific situation or circumstance.

In our business, everything should revolve around people—employees, guests, and other stakeholders. Showing a clear dedication to them, with a focus on learning about them through proper engagement, observation, and asking the right questions, a stellar professional in the people business will be able to utilize information to create unmatched moments that guests will never forget. I urge every leader to perfect this trade and learn about people, focus on their needs and wishes, see and learn about reactions and active outcomes, and always keep in mind that a true hotelier understands this trade better than anyone.

As people professionals, we are always challenged to create new MMs. It is a cycle that never ends: Every day brings new guests and fresh opportunities. Great leaders and organizations continuously exceed expectations through dedication, professionalism, and clear focus on the people, not only to do a job but because we as leaders are dedicated to others' well-being at all times.

Superior service is truly about going the extra mile. For instance, a housekeeper might observe that the guest's toothpaste is almost finished and simply replaces it. Furthermore, that housekeeper might see that a particular type of coffee has run out in the coffee station in the room and automatically adds more, along with a little note. The same thing can be done with water or anything else that a staff member observes in the room that the guest might need—all can be done without disturbance. A little handwritten note highlighting an extra touch then goes a long way. A customer sees and feels that the employee is a professional, is going above and beyond for their comfort, and this creates special moments for them. This is part of a solid corporate culture, where all employees understand the importance of creating memories and, therefore, customers for a lifetime.

2. THINK LIKE A GUEST (GUEST MINDSET):

To achieve and execute Memory Moments, to ensure that customers trust you, your brand, and your business, it is vital that employees and particularly leaders have the ability to think like a guest and to put themselves in the shoes of the customer—and become almost clairvoyant. True hoteliers and people professionals utilize this almost instinctual knowledge to create "customer surprises" with the right talents and understanding in how to execute them.

It takes time, effort, successes, as well as many failures to achieve consistent positive outcomes to actually begin to understand how guests feel, think, and act, but this expertise—a necessary innate talent—is invaluable for hoteliers. As we are in the people business, we understand what to look for, how to speak, what kind of questions to ask, how and when to engage and when to step back and observe. It is not only our job, but also a rewarding part of our profession to utilize this trade and to create a competitive advantage and ensure the clients become loyal to our hotel or brand. As a leader, it is vital to teach this important trade to employees—to see it in action and to model it—as they will be mostly responsible for creating unparalleled memories with each interaction, or at least to learn more about a guest by properly engaging anyone at any time.

It is always absolutely important to give a guest your full attention, using all your senses and creating that moment or instance where the guest feels that someone is there to create a feeling of security and comfort. Your professionalism, personal engagement, and empathy will help you to build trust with the guests, step by step. Remember, the customer should always be in the limelight; the employees are the supporting players who make the light shine on the guest even brighter. Professionals look for signs of what the guest needs without being intrusive. Every area of the hotel might be different. When the guest walks through the hotel, they might look around and be in search of something. The employee who is closest needs to decide that they are responsible for that guest. An employee needs to have a circle of action, which is a perimeter where that employee approaches and "owns" the guest, and by observing the behavior or body language, the employee will know how to approach that guest and ask the right question so they can assist properly and professionally.

For example, when a guest walks into the lobby at or before dinnertime, based on the signals the guest is giving, we might ask if they are joining us for dinner. "May I escort you to one of our restaurants?" During that walk, we can ask for their name and whether they have a reservation, then introduce them to the hostess of that particular place. It is always possible as well to exchange business cards, get more information from the guest, and perhaps learn if he or she is celebrating something special that evening. In that instance, that employee who greeted and feels responsible for the guest will then further delight that customer with a special surprise if she's celebrating a birthday or if we can find out a particular preference that the servers can then act upon. (For instance, the guest might indicate in conversation how they love Italian sparkling wine as an aperitif.)

Another example might be from the restaurant setting: A guest starts to cough. We might, without being asked, bring the guest a cup of hot water with lemon or honey and a little note from the server to wish them a speedy recovery. Furthermore, through conversation and the art of asking the right questions (with professionalism, confidence, happy to enchant) a server will be able to suggest particular dishes that might be soothing or healing for a cold, like a nice soup or a stew, without overstepping any boundaries.

As a patron in a restaurant, have you ever gotten up to find the restroom, looking wildly around past the bar, past the kitchen, for the right place to go? A professional in the people business, without making a guest feel uncomfortable, might see that guest get up and before they have to flag somebody down, and immediately step in and assist with escorting the guest to the bathroom discreetly.

In another setting: An unhappy guest is waiting in line for checkout and might look a little anxious. It is critical to identify them and, without asking, escort them to a special area to do the necessary paperwork. During the conversation, we might learn that they are behind schedule and need to attend an urgent meeting. Due to our attention and understanding of how to engage, we might call for a taxi in advance and ensure that the guest can depart on time. At a luxury hotel, we may even arrange for a driver if it is feasible. This could create a guest for life.

It's all about creating these memories. Let's say an airline has lost our guest's luggage. We ask if we can help fill their needs until their luggage arrives by perhaps bringing a tailor over to construct a skirt or a pair of pants that are ready by the next day. You blow people away with this. And then, when the luggage arrives, you leave it in the room with a little note "from" the luggage:

> *Hello, my dear. I'm sorry I kept you waiting. I made a little detour to Peru. I really didn't enjoy it because I wanted to be with you. And finally, we're together again*!

Then we put lavender in the envelope so the room smells heavenly and brings the blood pressure down naturally. Now the guest is so happy that somebody took the time to construct a cute little note for their missing luggage that they will remember this gesture fondly from our hotel, and we hopefully have made a guest for life.

3. MAKE QUALITY YOUR OWN (QUALITY MINDSET):

I am passionate about this topic, as creating quality products and services is the key goal of any organization. I learned a long time ago that I can only "win" my space in this industry if I master the approach to quality management and develop my own quality mindset.

What is quality and how is it defined? Probably most of your guests or customers have their own perception of quality. From my standpoint, quality is when they are provided with an exceptional product or service. In the people business we talk about the guest journey or guest experience. When we focus on a quality experience, there are several parts to take into consideration. Golder, Mitra, and Moorman stated in their 2012 study "What Is Quality? An Integrative Framework of Processes and States"[4] that a quality experience seen from the guest's standpoint focuses on the product or service through the lens of various measurements, including (a) knowledge, (b) motivation, (c) emotions, and (d) expectations. Guests will always judge the product or service through their lens of the expected "ideal."

All companies aim to achieve the highest possible customer satisfaction, which is a judgment of the guest comparing a consumed product or service to their expected level of an ideal experience. It is our task to ensure that quality comes to life in all areas of a hotel with the intent to achieve the best possible experience for the guest.

I often compare our approach with a tailor who measures the key parts of your body to come up with a "tailor made" suit, which fits only you. Furthermore, you personalize this suit with the fabric, the colors, and then you try to match and balance the look with particular accessories based on your tastes, your expectations, your ideal feel and look. When you tailor a suit, you have to try it on at least once, if not twice, to be absolutely sure that it fits you perfectly. In the hospitality business we need to adapt this approach through learning about the guest, identifying what motivates them, what is important in their comfort and likes and dislikes, and what makes them happy.

A final product or service should then match or exceed expectations to create that tailor-made experience. We have to learn how to ask the right questions at the right time, as will be illustrated in part two in "Communication." Through your expertise you try to get the information, which allows you to go above and beyond without intruding into the space of the guest but makes the customer feel special. Again, you know how to engage to create incomparable memories and to touch the heart of the guests.

In addition, quality means consistency at the highest possible level, and that is where "no breakdowns" come in to play. You and your team—the entire organization—need to understand the importance of quality and have processes in place to teach employees to be able to perform at that highest level. Quality needs to be ingrained as part of the entire corporate culture and how business gets done in an organization.

Like the metaphor of the Swiss watch, every component and every role needs to be executed flawlessly, exceeding guests' expectations. It is important to comprehend and see that every employee plays a crucial part in that creation and each person is as important as the other. As a leader, you have the opportunity and duty to ensure team members are inspired to learn and grow and to achieve more through your guidance. You lead the way, set the example and tone, and support the clear guidelines necessary to ensure sustainable success. The most important difference to any physical product is that in our business, the people business, the product is everything the guest sees, feels, consumes, touches, and hears. Our product is an experience, one that is personalized, creates positive emotions, touching the heart of the guest, custom-made to their needs, and presented in a most fascinating way.

In the United States, the Malcolm Baldridge Quality Award was created to formally recognize performance excellence of both public and private US organizations, given by the president of the United States. The first awards were handed out in 1988, and the first hospitality company to ever win was Ritz-Carlton in 1992, then again in 1999. I had the pleasure of being part of the company the second time around, which was an important learning journey for all employees, making us all better professionals in the process.

I would like you to think and live "quality" with everything you do. You have to create that mindset and let it become a part of how you live and how you behave and work. It is important to understand, own, and lead "quality" to achieve consistent improvements and get closer to perfection every single day. Quality in hospitality means that the service and products created and delivered to guests are free from deficiencies, in many ways tailor made, and presented in a way to charm and surprise the guests. Quality has to be part of every employee's "DNA" to ensure that each step of their work proceeds without any shortcomings and allows the guest to have a flawless and incredible experience. Everyone needs to live quality in every aspect of their job, in every interaction with guests or peers, and with a clear mindset and focus to create excellence in everything.

4. THINK BUSINESS (BUSINESS AND ENTREPRENEURIAL MINDSET):

As an expert or up-and-coming expert in your business, or as the title of the book indicates, as a "Master in Hospitality," the advice given through experience and research will no doubt help you to create a clear business mindset.

You always want to put on your business mindset hat when you wake up in the morning because that focus gives you a clear mission. Every new day is a great opportunity to improve your competencies—*you* decide how fast and how far you will go by how intent you are to achieve your own vision. Everything you do for your own growth will make you a better businessperson, as long as you have an open mind. You will become a respected professional who clearly understands what is most important and how to achieve sustainable business success.

You are at the core of your success. You are the one who can develop into the professional you always dreamed of being. You are the one who has all the cards in your hands to become successful as a leader and as a businessperson. You understand how to build and further develop your strengths and key areas, which make you the best that you can be. Follow the advice, the approach in this book, work hard on yourself, and you will excel in your job to achieve your goal. Always remember that you need to grow from the inside—from your core strengths (talents)—and then improve your competencies based on a clear vision and plan. You want to become the best professional that you can be, and this incorporates developing your business mindset in tandem with growing all your other skill sets. Professionalism is the key to success and growing through the ranks, and with your open mind and understanding the business mindset, you will become unbeatable.

I learned a long time ago that I needed to become a strategist, which means that every decision I make today, be it for my own growth or for the company I work for, will affect my own course and that of the business. In the same way you map out your own plan (as you'll do in part two on "The Eight Principles for Excellence in the People Business"), you'll bring a strategic approach to your goals and outcomes through clear objectives, actions, and road maps. Your overarching goal will always be to improve and further develop your overall business acumen, keeping an open mind to understand the different elements required and the impact of your decisions.

You'll focus on the positive and learn from the negative, turning those disappointments into future "wins." You'll always remember, as a top professional, that change is part of daily life, and you'll know how to make change your own and use it to achieve the best possible outcome. You'll learn how to adapt quickly to be competent, take the appropriate actions, and make the best decisions when something unexpected and new comes your way. Having a business mindset means thinking like an investor, owner, banker, and corporate executive who has to make a business financially viable and successful in the short-run as well as over the long-term.

MY DEFINITION OF A HOTELIER

When I put together the pieces that define a hotelier and not just a hotel manager, these are the traits I believe lead to success:

- Is a people professional
- Serves others
- Makes others feel special about themselves
- Demonstrates the highest standards for themself at all times
- Is authentic
- Is passionate
- Is humble
- Is empathetic
- Has integrity
- Is respectful
- Is curious
- Leads by example
- Is a constant learner
- Is quality driven
- Is courteous, gracious, and graceful
- Is curious about the world and its citizens
- Is self-motivating, with a desire to go above and beyond
- Exhibits an infectious sense of ease, warmth, and excellence
- Understands the business aspect of every action

The desired outcome of a competent hotelier is recognized by these traits:

- Has the aptitude to successfully manage the business.
- Builds trust and demonstrates strong leadership of self and others.
- Achieves desired financial and business results, both short- and long-term.
- Creates value consistently and for all stakeholders involved.
- Crafts an overall environment for all employees to achieve their full potential.

This list might sound different from what you've heard before. I believe the greatest achievement of a hotelier is to receive feedback from guests about the amazing experiences that were created for them by the employees at the hotel. Day in, day out, the people working with you and for you do a big part of the job, directly communicating and impacting a customer's experience.

As you strive for more senior leadership positions in the hotel industry, you will realize quickly how employees mirror your behavior, good or bad. Having spent most of my professional life in luxury hotels, I am always surprised to see managers, even top managers in their positions, who do not comprehend "leadership" properly and therefore don't lead by example. Not only in this industry, but in any business around the world, leaders should always aspire to become role models to their employees and everyone they encounter on a professional level.

You expect to see and experience your immediate managers, midlevel managers, and senior leaders, specifically the top leaders of any business, behaving based on the brand expectation and corporate culture. You want to measure them not just by what they say but by their actions. True leadership means you "walk the walk and talk the talk." You don't say words without unified action to back them up; empty rhetoric disconnects from your team(s) and decreases your credibility as leader.

DRESSING AND ACTING THE PART OF A HOTELIER

As hoteliers, we have to portray a professional image at all times. This starts with appearance—grooming. We must make sure that we follow the guidelines of the brand and portray an image based on our "own brand" as well, even bringing grooming to the next level. Yes, we all should become our own "fashion icons." The clothes we wear must be impeccable, with no wrinkles or stains, and our shoes must be polished and not scuffed. How we present ourselves matters. It's important to understand that the clothes you wear do not make you who you are; it's your personality that brings "the true you" to life and makes all the difference.

We create a look that fits in smoothly with our overall environment, but we stand out because of our personality, humbleness, and the way we portray ourselves. One important mentor explained to me that our job as people professionals and hoteliers is to be in the limelight, like on a movie set or a big stage, and our appearance is part of creating a flawless and smooth experience for our guests at all times.

Our words, our tone of voice, our body language, facial expressions, attire, and our attitudes—everything we say and do and, often more importantly, everything that we don't say speaks volumes to the many eyes looking to us for guidance. As such, our position is highly visible and our guests expect a certain image from us. We need to reflect the brand's promise to the guests, supporting and executing the overall mission and vision of the organization. It's important that your overall visual representation is part of who you are, that your personality allows you to express the authentic "you," so that you feel at ease at all times. If you feel natural, then the guests and the employees feel comfortable being with and around you. I'm asking you to show up as authentically as you can each day and be your very best consistently.

The role of a hotelier has many facets, and we must embody and portray the brand's model at all times. A leader needs to strive to become a role model for their employees—their team—and create that atmosphere where they are enthusiastic to do their best at all times, mirroring the boss's behaviors. In chapter five I will define for you in more detail what a true role model is. You are selected to be a role model by employees who value you for who you are, what you do, and how you do things. But it is important to remember that you are always a mentor, aspiring to be selected as a role model by the team members.

Every interaction should be individualized. It begins with a smile. You can say "Yes, but I smile at everybody." But I would argue that's not true. You don't smile at all people in the same way—it's all about creating synergy. If you have a good interaction with your guest, they'll remember it. This is essential to your business, as is learning how to make these moments stand out.

ETIQUETTE AND GOOD MANNERS

It is vital in our profession to understand how the elements of etiquette and manners apply in our daily lives and in various situations. Good manners is a general approach to treating other people with courtesy and giving of yourself. Etiquette is an understanding of how to behave in a specific situation, particularly while dining. In our business and throughout our journey through life, we will have many opportunities to dine out, entertain family, friends, and guests, and as a hotelier, you are expected to understand these principles.

The topic is important to me because I see in my travels around the world and with my own staff that this important "art" is often overlooked. Clearly every culture has its own "rules" and etiquette norms. Guests look at you in your role as a people professional, and might want to emulate you. Here are some simple guidelines you can practice without becoming "stiff," as you always want and need to blend in but with that extra know-how and politeness. The below info is more for a formal Western setting. Treating others with courtesy, kindness, and respect is an important part of a hotelier's foundation. The list below is not complete by far, and it's important to remember to adapt to the specific guidelines of the culture you're in and the significance of a particular meal:

- Seat the ladies first (expected from gentlemen only) and ensure you get up if the lady next to you needs to step out. This might seem like it's from out of an old playbook, and in many cultures this gesture has become obsolete. However, I strongly believe it demonstrates elegance and courtesy, and in more formal settings, you can't go wrong to rely on tradition.

- To the extent possible, ensure that you give enough space to the person on either side of you. Never intrude into their personal space.

- Place your napkin on your lap when you take your seat and use it as needed throughout the meal.

- Cutlery can be confusing, but the rule is simple: work your way outside in. After use, place the utensils on the plate for the servers to clear.

- While there are cultural differences here, in most settings you should bring the utensils to your mouth and not lower or bend your head to the plate. Never point with any eating utensil. And never talk with a full mouth.

- When you are not eating, try to place the palms of your hands touching the edge of the table. And never put your elbows on the table.

- Maintain proper upright posture throughout.

- Refrain from using your mobile phone, as the focus should be on the conversation at the table. You do not want to give the impression that your mobile device is more important than the guests. Simply turn it off.

- If you have to sneeze, always use your own clean white handkerchief, neatly folded, and turn away from the table, away from anyone, and be silent. Apologize if it disturbs others. If you have to get up, respectfully excuse yourself from the table.

- Only touch the wine or champagne glass at the stem; this shows elegance and understanding about wine.

- After the meal, fold your napkin and place it to the left of your setting.

- When getting up, help the person next to you by pulling their chair out, and let them leave the table first (primarily for gentlemen assisting others). Then push their chair back into the original position.

- Always thank the host and let her or him leave the room before anyone else.

I am fascinated by this topic, and it is critical for you to learn and understand it. I want you not only to be comfortable but also to be able to demonstrate discreetly to others what etiquette is all about, while always respecting and adhering to cultural and local expectations and norms.

UNDERSTANDING YOUR SPECIFIC ROLE

What is your role as a junior manager, supervisor, or senior leader in achieving the desired strategic goals, financial expectation of ownership and the hotel company? You play a critical part in creating that competitive advantage to improve the overall quality of service and products through your professionalism, drive for excellence, passion for people, and by working hard to create unmatched memories for your fellow employees and guests. Your role as a leader or future leader is to become the best that you can be at your current job, to set the example, and lead your coworkers to sustainable success. They will thank you by working hard and by demonstrating pride and joy with every action.

Please remember that leadership is not about the title you hold, but walking your talk. Every single employee needs to become a business leader, understanding the why and what of the company, the owner and operator expectations to ensure total alignment in the approach to take care of both employees and guests, and to achieve the desired business results.

You are part of an organization that relies on your contributions and your daily support in order to achieve the vision and mission of your company. The sooner you start thinking like a general manager or a business owner, the better you will grasp your job scope and can contribute to the desired success in a professional and consistent manner. As you may now better understand, consistency is paramount. I suggest you step up in every possible moment to learn, serve others, listen and observe, and improve your competencies and leadership abilities. This approach will help you get used to leading others by setting the example, working hard to assist team members to succeed as you move a step closer to your ultimate goal.

LEARNING TO CONTROL YOUR EMOTIONS AND REACTIONS AS A HOTELIER

As a top professional and a hotelier, you need to watch yourself closely, especially what you say and do in front of others. You are in control of your own emotions, and you need to clearly understand the impact your emotions will have on someone else.

Emotions are important—but only if controlled. The best bosses who made a lasting impression on me took their time to explain a certain issue or concern they had with me, away from other people, in private, and never in front of anyone else. The critical learning from this was not about the particular mistake but how this leader took the time to teach me, to build me up positively, in a professional and controlled manner. As a leader, you achieve your goals when you have an employee walk away from a situation feeling and becoming more competent, inspired to work harder, better, faster, smarter.

You need to get your message across to employees in a positive and constructive way. This practice is called "constructive criticism." You need to offer a valid and well-reasoned opinion about the work or concern of your employee, involving both positive and negative comments in a friendly way. If not, you lose your credibility as a leader, and you might even lose your employees' trust, particularly as a mentor. Yes, you can raise your voice to a certain level, but it must always be restrained and with the right outcome in mind. You need to be in command of the message, and you have to live with the reactions of your team members. It is necessary to show concern about an issue, but if your level of agitation gets out of control, others may lose respect for you. I'm telling you this so you do *not* fall into this trap.

Throughout your career, you will never forget the people who impacted you negatively, and often you'll even remember their names and exactly where you were when you were scolded or reprimanded. These experiences will stay with you forever; it's like you click a special button to recall bad memories, which should remind you not to act in the same way. These less-than-optimal past experiences are what I call lifelong teaching moments—they shape you and remind you not to repeat these less-than-stellar performances.

I want you to have a proactive approach when you face challenges or a person who might be difficult. This will help you as well when you face an upset guest. Take a deep breath before you speak.

This simple practice allows a necessary pause and gives you time to make a conscious response, no matter how challenging the circumstance. Always keep the focus on the desired outcome.

When you put yourself into somebody else's shoes, it's an effective way to get into their mind, particularly while in discussions as a team, while in a one-on-one with an employee, your supervisor, or with that difficult guest who is angry and wants to complain to you. The angry guest who is upset over a minor issue might seem like he's being unreasonable over a room assignment, but this might have been a very long day for him. Perhaps his flight was delayed or his daughter was sick in the middle of the night. Maybe his luggage was lost, his boss yelled at him, or he has a new deadline he doesn't know how he's going to meet, and he was looking forward to being able to look out at the sea view he had booked and not at the tennis courts. When you look at his exasperation through his eyes, you know not to take his huffiness personally and to do your best to lighten the guest's mood through professional behavior, showing empathy, and trying to make that experience a better one.

Oftentimes, guests just want to be listened to and to feel important, but you have the ability and hopefully the empowerment to decide what is best for that guest to ensure you can win over this guest for life. You, as a top professional, understand the particular need and can act accordingly.

You might have already, or will face more challenging employee situations in the future. I would like you to approach them in a similar way. It is always critical to understand the employee first, to give them an opportunity to speak up, explain the situation in a professional environment, where you put that staff member at ease. As I learned from Stephen Covey, "seek first to understand, then to be understood." It was a valuable lesson then, and it still is today.

It is vital to show that you as a leader try to clearly get to the bottom of the concern, through the eyes of the employees and through getting facts from others based on the circumstance. You owe it to anyone to lend an ear, be professional, and not to make rushed conclusions before clearly understanding and weighing the various points of view. Document the conversation and be consistent with the policies of the company and the way you communicate with an employee, regardless of the situation. Certain employee discussions require a third party as witness. Please follow the guidelines of your organization. Throughout the entire discussion with that employee, keep an open and fair mind and never jump to premature conclusions.

Sometimes these types of conversations can lead to more serious consequences for the employee, and therefore, you want to weigh all points clearly and follow the procedures accordingly. In the end you want to be confident that the outcome is clear for both parties and that you have done your utmost to solve an issue in the best interest of both parties.

Remember that you always want to manage the situation and not let the situation manage you. You want and need to be able to keep yourself focused and determined on the best possible and most fair outcome, but remain open and flexible in the way to get there, particularly with guest issues. Be creative in how you solve problems. We'll be talking about creativity later in principle #5, "Build and Strengthen Your Core Competencies."

Great leaders empathize and intuitively understand the reactions of their actions. Every time you say something, you can either improve people's trust and confidence in you, or decrease trust and cause worry about your competence. Remember that every action has a consequence that potentially affects people, the hotel, the brand, and you either positively or negatively.

Now that we have a better understanding of what it means to be a hotelier, next we will find out the steps it takes to achieve your dream career in this most rewarding business.

CHAPTER FIVE
THE PATH TO SUCCESS:
ACHIEVING YOUR DREAM CAREER

To handle yourself, use your head;
to handle others, use your heart.
—Eleanor Roosevelt

I encourage both young and established hoteliers to dream big about your career. No one can tell you that you are not good enough for any of your desired goals. Show yourself first that you can achieve your dreams, and prove everyone wrong who was ever in doubt about you. A career can be planned to a certain point, but it must be supported by a willingness to work harder than others, a determination to succeed, and a desire to become the best that you can be. These are all critical to your future success. And once you have the basics down, the most important factor is to work with the right company, with leaders who have your best interests in mind, and with mentors who will go above and beyond to teach you and lead you to greater heights. Get ready to fly.

GETTING STARTED IN YOUR CAREER

As I wrote in chapter one, the first time I worked in a hotel was when I had just returned from my English learning experience in the United States. I had spoken with a local hotelier close to my home, and he invited me to start working at the front desk. It was a small hotel, but it was exciting and interesting to meet all the customers, to talk with them, to be able to check them into their hotel rooms smoothly, to take care of their requests, and to be part of this hotel team. The staff was wonderful, warm, and friendly. I could see then that every team member enjoyed working there, that they all respected the general manager because of his kindness, genuineness, and because he had a knack for being able to make the staff feel good about the work we were doing. Even in stressful situations, I felt supported, although sometimes I experienced the general manager's dissatisfaction if I made the occasional mistake or two.

This experience gave me great hands-on training, but my ambition to be the best, and to get the preferred practice and theoretical expertise meant I worked hard to get into École Hotelière de Lausanne (EHL). My journey to enter and then graduate from "EHL" was important to me, long but full of excitement. After my local hotel experience, I made a list of items and important steps to get to the interview stage at the prestigious hotel school. At that time, the lessons were taught in French, and I absolutely needed to improve my language capabilities in order to be accepted into EHL. I knew I had to work hard to gain more basic hotel experience and then to learn the French language properly. It was critical to find a hotel in the French-speaking part of Switzerland.

I was excited to receive an opportunity in a locally managed property at Lake Geneva. This was a crucial accomplishment that allowed me to become more focused and professional through both my tenacity and consistent commitment to achieve excellence. After graduating from EHL, I received a great offer I could not refuse, becoming the #2 in that same hotel with my first mentor, and I continued my great learning journey under his wings. After a period of two years, and with some savings, it was time to "conquer" the world and continue my growth by learning from the best. Armed with what I thought was a great résumé, I sought out the most renowned hotels in the world to pursue my quest to attain my dream job.

For any young and future hotelier who does not have the opportunity to join a hotel school, I want to say that the way to your dream job is equally wide open. As I stated earlier, I have encountered top professionals who have achieved a general manager job through hard work, going through the "ranks" with the right mental approach, focus, a company that supports growth from within, creating learning tools to support their own vision, and competent leadership and mentorship.

The lesson I want you to take away is simple. Whether you are joining a company for your first job, are just coming out of hotel school, or are in your midcareer, join an organization that has a solid corporate culture and corporate values that are practiced by all—including senior leadership—on a daily basis and that is respected by guests and stakeholders alike. You want to be able to trust that people above you do more for you than for themselves, have only the best in mind for you, and who demonstrate leadership, commitment, and excellence in everything they do. Don't waste your time with people who love to talk more than they actually accomplish tasks or achieve goals, leaders who think they are good but cannot demonstrate it, or people who put their own needs above the rest.

I urge you to study your future company well. Nowadays you have many more tools at your disposal compared with twenty years ago. Use them wisely: interact with the people who work there, go on social media, get feedback, visit the property prior if you can, and ensure that you feel comfortable based on your own goals and desires, your natural fit based on your talents and growth path.

I was looking to fine-tune my overall skills based on the highest possible standards in the industry. I researched various hotels and companies and came to the conclusion that a big important city in the United States was the best option for me at that time. I was looking for leadership, service, and product greatness, like-minded people in the same organization who strive for the best, incorporated and continually fine-tuned processes, and a company who could take employees to the next level and not only hire people, but select employees for future, bigger roles in the organization. So I narrowed my list, did as thorough research as I could at that time, got feedback from the few people I knew who could help, and prepared myself to send out letters for potential interviews. I asked myself, What is their brand? What are they known for? What is their signature flair?

To become a leader in your profession, you want to learn from the best. This is a crucial point in how to choose your future employer. It has guided me throughout my career. I strongly believe that you can find excellence in many hotels around the world, and—most importantly—select that hotel based on both your ability to learn there and to add value to the organization through your contributions.

There has been a lot of consolidation in the marketplace when it comes to hotels, with many larger brands acquiring smaller ones, so they now encompass multiple price points. For instance, the largest hotel companies in the world have more than thirty brands in their portfolio, ranging from simpler roadside hotels to luxury brands.

It's important to look at the opportunities offered at your potential place of employment, the corporate culture, how you could potentially fit within, the diversity in these brands, their training programs, their benefits, and most importantly, your passion to grow to the highest possible level in any brand of that organization.

Once you are ready and believe it is the moment to contact that company for a potential opportunity, it's time to prepare for the best first impression. Some hotel companies simply require you to go online and follow the necessary steps to apply, while others might expect you to contact them via email or whatever means they demand. Here comes a very important part. You have to showcase who you are—your authenticity, strengths, professional goals—through a top professional presentation, email communication, or whatever means it requires. You have the possibility here to shine through your first impression. I must tell you, as someone who has selected hundreds of employees in my career, you want to portray the best image you can. Get help with your preparation if you need it in order to present your message in a way that distinguishes your from others in the best and most authentic way possible.

When you make it to the interview, you've already passed an important stage. This refers not only to those applying for their first hotelier job but also to many of you who are already in an organization but seeking a further career move. This approach applies to everyone who is looking to change, for whatever reason.

THE INTERVIEW AND THE OFFER: WHAT TO CONSIDER

You may remember the story from chapter one of how brusquely I was treated by several companies I was interviewing with in New York and how that really made a negative impression on me. How different it was when I met with the company I ultimately ended up working for, where I was warmly greeted. The latter experience made all the difference in the world to me because their company values came shining through. This is the time to take in everything you can about the company, from beginning to end, from how you are greeted, to the employees who meet with you, the questions you are asked, the type of interview process you go through. Was it thoughtful? Did you feel like your time was well spent? Were you impressed with the people you met? Were you asked intelligent questions? What kind of materials were you handed—what did they want you to know about their company and the opportunities they have for your career and your growth?

I mention all of this because you want to be chosen based on who you are and what you can bring to the organization. On the other hand, you want to know that the organization and leaders have the best in mind for your career, which might not be easy to identify initially, depending on the position, but it should become clearer based on the leaderships' support for career growth and indications of employees moving up the ladder and being promoted into senior roles.

When we meet with new graduates of hotel schools, we congratulate them for their degree. I want to know what they learned, why they are in the business, their ultimate goal, and what they would like to do as a first job after graduation. Oftentimes, people don't really know what they want. "I want to be a manager," they say. For a longer-term goal, this might be the right direction, but it still doesn't indicate a clearly thought out career path. In addition, this indicates that they have not been prepared well by their college, because no one ever becomes a manager straight out of school. We have to explain what the reality is: they will be in a management support role or perhaps in a simpler full-time entry-level role. It is important to receive enough practical basic training to create a solid foundation, allowing for an eventual move up the ladder.

This is where the credibility of the school comes into play, because the teachers and people in charge of the school should have better prepared the student for the normal course of a career path. For instance, I have often been asked about how we select the best person for the job. This is a more and more important question, as highly skilled employees become increasingly rare due to the fast pace of hotel developments going up around the world. The best and most proven approach is to focus on the strengths of any candidate.

We want to select a future leader or executive, not someone who just fills a temporary "void" in the organization. We want to ensure that the questions you are asked focus on your talents, so that you can give us examples about who you are, what drives you, what motivates you, how you learn best, what you have contributed to other teams, and what contributions you have made to help your fellow employees become better workers. I'm looking to identify your core talents and natural enthusiasm for a potential job within my hotel.

A hotel or company will not invest in mediocrity, as it simply would not make business sense. If you invest your own money in the stock market, would you want to buy in to a losing company?

Probably not. This is the same for organizations when they make decisions to invest in their human capital. They expect an appropriate return, which means that you as an employee can make a difference in your position and your company's standing compared to any competitor. You are the key to any hotel company's success (or any organization for that matter), and they expect you to contribute positively to achieve long-term growth.

I know that important questions for anyone joining a company or moving to the next stage in their career are what is the salary and what benefits are offered. Of course salary is critical, but perhaps it's not the most important thing in your decision to join or move to another position. In fact, many studies have shown that money by itself is not the primary motivator for happiness or success. If you are focused on solid career-building, you may make a transition to a company that is a better fit for you, taking a short-term sacrifice in your salary or a lateral move if a promotion is not yet viable for you. Or, ideally, you will earn your next promotion through your efforts, hard work, and contributions. This principle has guided me throughout my career. A great organization will always pay you fairly and based on the competition, but there is more to it. Learning and growing does not have a price tag, but it is the ticket to a successful career.

I read a statistic somewhere about the growth in salary and benefits of working people around the world. The focus was on people with full-time jobs who had worked for a period of thirty-five years (on average) and was based on their first salary from a paying job and ending with their salary, benefits, potential stock options, etc., prior to retirement. The professionals fell into three categories. In the first category, people had an increase of about 300 to 500 percent of their salary and benefits over their lifetime. The second category had a 500 to 1,000 percent increase, and the last one was the professionals who grew their salary and benefits by more than 1,000 percent. I strongly believe that if you focus on your strength, your vision, your plan, along with everything I communicate with you in this book, you will exceed that 1,000 percent growth.

You are reading this book for a reason. You want to be the best that you can be. Being the best requires that you earn what you are worth. *Dream big, build your career properly, and you will enjoy the big benefits.* I want to make it clear that this calculation is only for your understanding and not to guide you in your various professional steps. I include it to show how it could be when all aspects of your life—profession, growth, and happiness—are in line. You will achieve completeness only when you build your career based on your own goals and vision, personally and professionally, and in the appropriate and most rewarding way.

Many people might shy away from jobs that are not considered easy, or locations that might be considered difficult. But you need to see there's a price for missing out on such opportunities: what you would have learned by taking on the more difficult task. It's good to have an opportunity where you can grow from your mistakes, and those naturally come from being put in a more challenging environment and even position. If you want to end up in Paris, you might need to go through Timbuktu, because there's never a direct way to your ideal location. But on the other hand, going through Timbuktu will make you stronger, and you will definitely learn things you probably never would have if you had taken a direct path to glory. So you should never shy away from opportunities, even if they don't sound like the perfect glamorous fit at the time.

STARTING YOUR NEW JOB

Once you are selected, as a new employee, you need to learn about the company firsthand—prior to starting to work in any function. The company, mostly the human resources leaders, have a great opportunity to showcase the hotel at this point to ensure you understand the vision and mission and get to know the key people of the hotel (which is absolutely crucial, so that they get to know you and you feel comfortable engaging with the senior leadership). This onboarding experience is a process to ensure the employees feel how important they are to the organization and for the company to create that long-lasting bond.

As a new employee, you will encounter many hardworking people already in their jobs or positions for some time. A majority of them might have never had the chance to join a hotel school, having earned their knowledge and position through commitment and dedication every single day. They learned their craft from the ground up, and I have always admired them for their relentless drive to achieve professional excellence in what they do. They become extremely important mentors for others and can guide and direct through an authentic approach to the business or tasks on hand. I want to be sure to emphasize this point, as it's extremely important to me—the hotel industry is very egalitarian in this way.

There are many examples out there of leaders who have the ability to capture others through their competencies and proven track record. There are natural leaders who have demonstrated excellence consistently, but I also strongly believe through both my research and personal experience that leaders can be made. The best leaders are the ones who've experienced the business from the ground up and have grown through the ranks with the right support and commitment from senior leaders.

MOVING UP THE LADDER OF SUCCESS

For those of you who are at the beginning of your careers, it's imperative to know that the journey to the top is long but extremely rewarding, exciting, enjoyable, as well as fun (most of the time). There is no shortcut to excellence! Every day you come to work, you can improve on your excellence. Step by step, you should have a plan in place for your growth, potential next steps, and hopefully the right leadership and mentors around you who are eager to see you succeed. True leaders have your best outcome in mind at all times, and if you feel that this is not the case, please voice your concerns directly with the people who can make a difference (not with any coworkers, which can create a bad work environment and start rumors).

Many companies offer great training and learning opportunities for all employment levels. Enroll in courses that can help you to achieve your goals. Sometimes leadership determines who can join those trainings. As someone who is eager to grow your career, you always want to be on that list. You'll achieve this by working hard and smart, by taking on additional responsibilities and doing more than others. Show at all times that you are eager and excited to work hard, first for your own sake and career growth and naturally for the company and leaders who have placed trust in your abilities. (I will elaborate on this important point in "Build and Strengthen Your Core Competencies" and "Continuous Education," principles #5 and #8 of "The Eight Principles for Excellence in the People Business.")

One of the key criteria of your personal growth is to establish a solid growth plan together with your leader or mentor. Various companies do a fantastic job with this, mainly because they need internal candidates to grow their business—eventually helping shareholder value. A healthy company creates great opportunities for you; these organizations will make sure that you can grow based on your own input, drive, and company opportunities. You want to make sure that you are part of a company that takes employee growth seriously, by communicating this important element in their basic company culture and value system.

In life, and particularly in your career, you want to take certain risks to advance according to your goals and time frame, but you need to weigh them carefully as well. When I made certain decisions both from my heart and for my professional journey, I always tried to align them with who I am in my core values, in my vision and mission, and in my own personal brand (see part two, principle #1). You have to feel good about what you do. I want you to be happy in your endeavor to create greatness for yourself. Nobody knows better than you who you are and who you would like to become. This self-knowledge has helped me to know that I wanted to travel the world but also helped me focus on every career step based on a clear path aligned with my heart and mind. To achieve sustainable success, you want to have a well-defined idea of your path to the future, and you will strive better, and potentially even faster, when you choose your next job based on your plan and your own unique brand.

I want you to reflect on some simple questions when you are at a crossing point. They are as follows:

1. Will the next job help me to utilize my skills?

2. Does the company's culture fit my own value system?

3. Will my next job allow me to be surrounded by people who can teach and inspire me?

4. Does my next job give me the opportunity to further my career and based on my own vision and mission?

These questions are only examples and require your further input so you can understand whether this potential career move is a great opportunity, or if other options woud suit you better.

FINDING AND CONNECTING WITH MENTORS AND ROLE MODELS

I believe that leaders grow through great mentors. Working on your career, at every step along the way, you want to have a mentor who is focused on your growth, who knows enough about you to be able to identify your strengths and weaknesses and understands your motivation and potential. A mentor is someone who can teach and guide you to achieve your own goals and dreams. You do not always have the opportunity to choose your mentor, but if you communicate your intentions and aspirations properly, you can ask your human resources department to match you with a mentor that you think is appropriate for your continuous growth.

A role model, on the other hand, is someone you can look up to, who you would like to become and simply admire from afar because of their knowledge, overall presence, business acumen, leadership capabilities, and successes. You should guide yourself based on an "ideal" leader who earned their status of a true role model. During my career and early years in the business, apart from my late father, I had César Ritz as one of my first role models. César Ritz was a Swiss hotelier who redefined luxury accommodation in Europe. He founded the Ritz in Paris and managed the Carlton Hotel in London, among others. Even though he died well before I was born, I admire his style, his business acumen, his relentless drive to improve our business, his innovative spirit, and the legacy he left. I was lucky enough to meet key executives of the best hotel company in the world who I looked up to for their drive, competency, and overall achievements and who I was able to have as mentors during several stages in my career. I was lucky to have "two in one"—a mentor who became my role model.

Not enough attention and focus is given to mentorship and role models, and not everyone who tries to be such a person actually succeeds. Unfortunately, there are too many less-than-satisfactory examples throughout organizations, resulting in less-than-happy employees and mediocre performances overall. I make this point particularly for our business, as I have seen too many mediocre leaders who thought they were great mentors. The worst is that they believed they were role models who employees actually looked up to. Organizations have weaknesses when analyzing and choosing mentors from within.

You, as a future leader, mentor, and hopefully a role model for others, know that you have to gain the acumen and respect from your peers and leaders through hard work and commitment to excellence every day. A good leader and mentor likes to be challenged and is there to support you. You, as an aspiring top professional, need to remain hungry to learn and not accept mediocrity. It is a relationship of respect and one that should grow.

Be ready to soak in new information at all times. When your mentor explains ideas to you, write them down immediately on a piece of paper or make a note on your cell phone. (The problem with using cell phones is that you get distracted easily and you might seem unfocused. Let the person know you are taking a few notes to avoid that impression.) If you do not understand, please ask. Sort your notes and feedback based on particular topics. You should be able to write your own book of excellence and keep adding to it. You will be able to refer back to your notes at any time, further elaborate on them, then translate them into actions you can take in your daily business life.

Many organizations underestimate the power of mentorships, yet research has outlined the importance of the mentorship role in creating a sustainable value system that further drives the commitment of individuals to achieve common goals. I believe companies have the responsibility to invest their money and time in competency building through mentors and role models, which helps build expertise throughout the organization leading to desired results. A mentor will be measured by their actions and expertise, not just by their words. That's why I ask you to challenge or question your mentor to ensure you understand their message and comprehend the entire picture.

I strongly believe that your environment plays a crucial role in your growth. Ideally, you want to be surrounded by people who model the right behavior and lead by example for you to naturally adapt and learn from the best. You grow through observing them—the way they conduct themselves, how they set the tone, and how they behave, communicate, and execute tasks.

In the end, translate what you learn from your mentor and role model into an approach that feels right for your personality.

KEEPING BALANCE AND LEARNING ABOUT THE WORLD AS YOU GROW YOUR CAREER

Oftentimes during my journey as a hotelier, I needed to pause to reflect on other things in life and ensure that I had the right state of mind to continue on this path to meet my professional goals. It is important that you follow your desires and ambitions to achieve the needed balance between work, family, and free time.

You have to find out for yourself what will make you happy, engaged, fulfilled, and well balanced. Try new things: sports, music, going to the theater, learning new skills, photography—whatever enriches and uplifts you. It's absolutely critical to have that balance of time outside of work to succeed in the long run. Don't forget that a hobby or a new skill can only help you with your professional journey. I never stopped my boxing and gym time, at least during three evenings a week. Furthermore, I play the trumpet, even if it is for only fifteen minutes every other day. It not only helps me to relax, but it feeds my passion for music.

Make sure to have wonderful and important moments with your loved ones, without any distractions and stress. Turn off your mobile phone and dedicate yourself to spending joyful hours with them. They need you and you definitely need them. Family is the most important gift you have. It is up to you to make them happy. During my career, I always set time aside to communicate with my parents and my brother back home in Switzerland. It was, and still is, absolutely critical for me to show my love to them, even if only through the phone or via Skype, but they need to know that I miss and love them. I go back home twice a year to be with them, to travel, to experience new cities, and to simply appreciate them, as they have given me the opportunity to become who I am today. Those moments are priceless to me. They make me more focused and happy to know that they are always with me.

You want to stimulate all your senses and grow through those new experiences. A hotelier needs to be comfortable in all different situations. One way to remain on top of your game is to constantly renew your knowledge on different aspects of life. For me, reading about the global economy and politics is important for my overall understanding of the world and their potential impacts on the business.

Another way of constantly improving is to show interest in our business by reading articles and books about our profession, be it in the world of food and beverage, or any other areas of the hotel business, because you want to be at the forefront of the innovations happening in our profession. There is always time for a good article, book, or discussion with peers, managers, and other top professionals. Make the internet your learning tool and fine-tune your ability to research using your curiosity and your drive to find answers to many questions. This process has allowed me to become more knowledgeable about many subjects that concern us as a whole, such as history and its natural cycles, the world of finance, art, and music, learning more about the connectedness of the world, as well as all the opportunities and the challenges the world brings. My approach and knowledge have helped me to be more calm as a person and a professional, as I understand better how to connect the dots with issues arising around myself.

Invest your free time wisely, enjoy your friends and family, and make yourself a better complete professional.

PART TWO

THE EIGHT PRINCIPLES FOR EXCELLENCE IN THE PEOPLE BUSINESS

CHAPTER SIX
INTRODUCING THE
EIGHT PRINCIPLES

Good leaders must first become good servants.
—Robert K. Greenleaf

The Eight Principles for Excellence in the People Business is a combination of the critical aspects of personal, professional, and company-focused expertise needed to ensure that you can achieve leadership excellence. When combined, strengths in each of these key areas allow a leader to create personal and professional successes.

During my doctoral journey, I had the opportunity to study hundreds of research papers, websites, and books in the areas of leadership, organizational excellence, personal development, training, coaching, and the luxury hotel business and how they all contribute to leadership excellence and organizational sustainability. I created this comprehensive framework to allow you to have a ready-made approach to enhance your own leadership excellence.

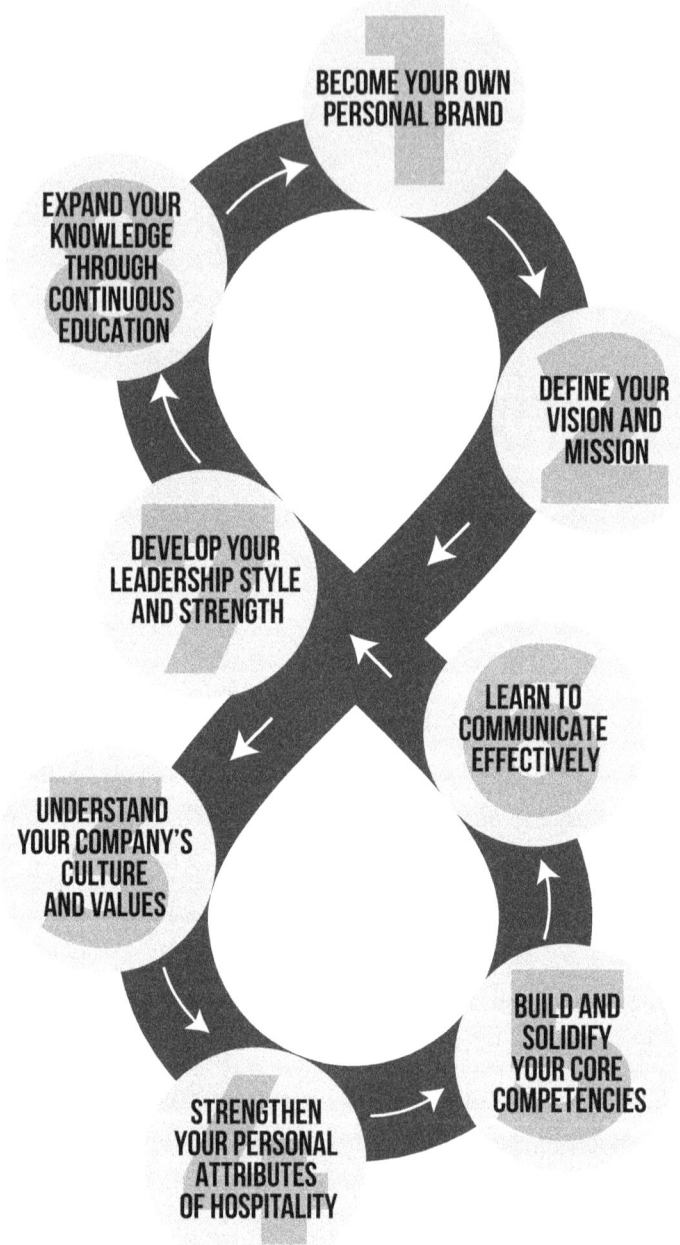

I use the metaphor of the number eight for the "eight principles." It represents how all eight elements combine to create a never-ending motion (infinity), which leads to personal and professional strength and sustainable success. Every principle plays a crucial role, is critical in itself, but they become powerful and indestructible when they all align perfectly and flow together in the same direction and motion. Also, the number eight means "infinity," "unbreakable," "success," and in the Chinese culture the number eight is the luckiest because it sounds like 發 (fa), which means "wealth," "fortune," and "prosperity."

It's my aim to assist you in your growth and to ensure that companies implement the right approach and tools to achieve sustainable success. You are the key to any company's success, and I hope you can establish yourself as that invaluable asset within any organization. You establish yourself through your own input, focus, and dedication to success, in combination with your employer's determination to build on your strengths, abilities, drive, know-how, and desire to become the best you can be.

Throughout my professional and academic journey, I've learned that leadership success starts with us—the people professionals. You have to take full responsibility for your achievements or failures but understand as well that there are other critical elements that need to be combined to create long-term success for you. For instance, you can be a solid leader, but if you are in the wrong environment, you might never succeed. Or you might not be a good leader yet, but with the right effort to build your communication skills and personal brand, you can achieve measurable improvements. Or you might work in an organization that has a solid culture and value system, but if you do not focus on your own growth, your development will suffer and you might not be able to contribute as expected, therefore never growing as a professional or a leader in that organization.

Even if you have all the right ingredients—where you work hard, focus on personal and professional growth, have a clear vision for yourself, work in an organization where the company culture is important, but your direct leaders do not adhere to the key elements of the company and value system, your growth might be substantially limited. Without solid leadership support, you will not be able to achieve your highest potential and eventually will fail in your quest to become the best. This will affect your ability to grow sustainably and will negatively impact the success of your organization.

There should be a mutual success agreement between you and your employer, where there needs to be a promise between you. Your career grows with leadership support, competency building through trainings and additional responsibilities, and the company will achieve success through your commitment, dedication, and professional input.

My aim is to assist you with a comprehensive approach to guiding your success, utilizing my research and my years of time spent serving in many countries around the world and assisting and leading thousands of employees to success. I was fortunate to learn from the best, and that is what I want for you as well.

You dictate the speed by working on the principles at your own pace, executing all of them, getting others involved if necessary, and constantly improving upon them.

Of course, every success comes with struggles and potential concerns and issues. Please know that as long as you attend to the eight principles of this framework in equal and consistent measure, you will achieve your desired goals. As you build your knowledge, competencies, and confidence, you will grow as a person and a professional in full alignment with your own vision and expectation.

There will be other influences determining your success, but you do not want to waste your time on issues and concepts that you cannot influence yourself. The key elements of the Eight Principles are all in your immediate circle of influence, even if you believe that some elements, like the corporate culture, are not directly within your responsibility.

You want to choose your employer wisely to ensure you create the best possible outcome for yourself. You are not "married" to one company for the rest of your life—it must be a mutually satisfying relationship. You want to focus on your growth together with the organization, the people in charge who can give you what you are looking for in terms of your own growth, your desired outcome, and based on your goals and dreams. Perhaps you want to be your own boss and want to become independent, which I would absolutely admire you for. You have it in your power to create the environment best suited to your desired success, leading others based on the highest expectations and on a culture that you create, shape, and live every day.

I want you to have confidence in your abilities and create that future you always dreamed of. Yes, it is possible to achieve anything you desire, with the right focus, understanding, determination, guidance, support, and a strong will to succeed.

CHAPTER SEVEN

PRINCIPLE #1: BECOME YOUR OWN PERSONAL BRAND

*People do not care how much you know
until they know how much you care.*
— John C. Maxwell

Your personal brand is all about who you are and what you represent. In this section of the book, I want you to spend time evaluating yourself, similar to a 360 degree review, to gain a better understanding of your talents, strengths and weaknesses, and focus on what you want to become known for. This is both a reflection on you now and an aspiration of your future self. I believe that developing a solid personal brand based on your natural talents, desires, and a clear understanding of what motivates you, will help keep you excited about all your next steps, both personally and professionally. You are unique and for this simple reason, you already stand out.

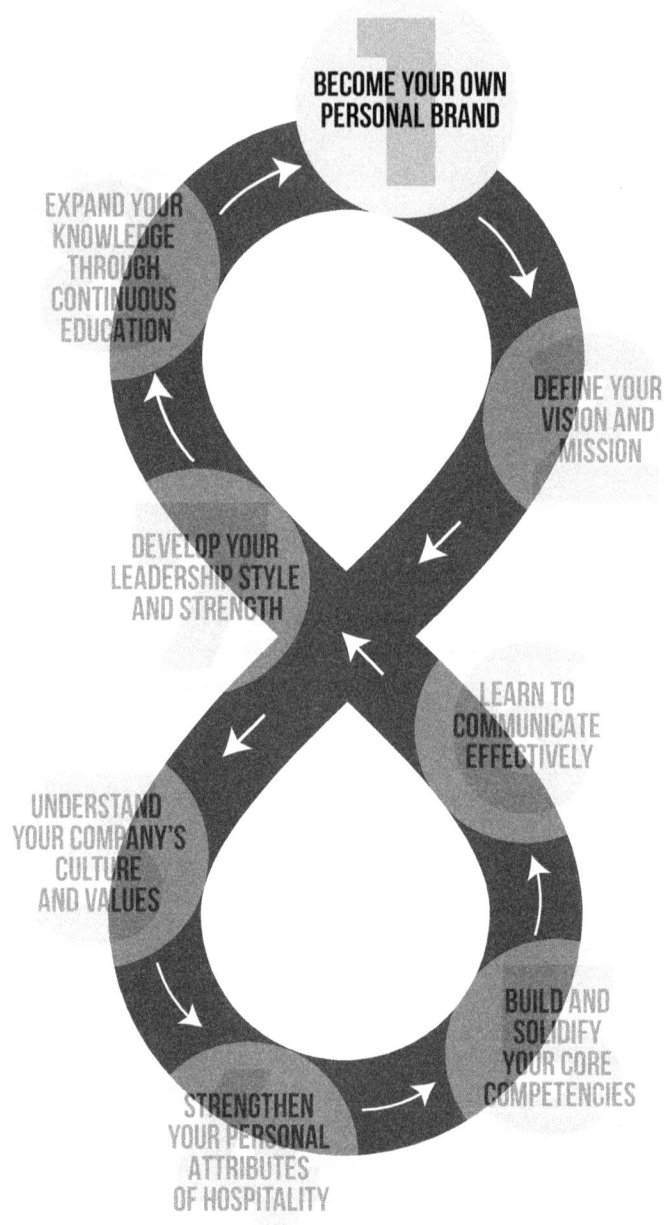

Remember, nobody can be you better than you! I would like you to go deeper, look at yourself from different angles, and then start to further develop and fine-tune these different areas to achieve your full potential. It is important to be self-critical, listen to others as well as yourself, and fully embrace your past successes.

Think about your personality and the impact you have on people. What is your broad emotional and practical appeal for others? Here are a few areas that might spark some ideas:

- What skills are you bringing with you to work every day?
- Are you known for your bright and cheery personality?
- Are you on time for work every day?
- Do you have a great sense of style that others comment upon?
- Do you inspire others when they are down or need support?
- Do you bring good ideas to the table at meetings?
- Do you have great empathy toward others?
- Do you have amazing people skills? Are you able to talk to almost anyone from any background?
- Are you making others better because of your desire for their growth?
- What comes naturally and easily to you?
- What makes you joyful and happy?

Next, open your ears and learn from what others say about you. Are you somebody your colleagues want on their team? Are they excited to work with you? People will judge you not just by what you say, but through your overall presentation and actions. People measure you not because you know everything, but because you help others to become more knowledgeable, instilling confidence in them through your actions.

You will gain respect from others because they like to listen when you speak, they appreciate learning from you, and because they admire who and how you are around others. You have to earn trust and respect from others, and you want your colleagues to be excited to be around you, your energy, and your ideas.

Now it's time to identify your personal core values. Some of them might be fairness, trust, being a good citizen, creativity, autonomy, authenticity. What really matters to you? Is it family? Travel? Financial success? What do you stand for?

Identify your passions. What do you love to do? What makes you excited when you get out of bed in the morning to come to work? What is something that you really enjoy and that you do very well? Is it engaging with guests, motivating your colleagues, coming up with new business ideas, trying out new foods, or problem solving? Some people love to go, go, go all day long while others like to be in a quiet room to think. What makes you tick? What's the perfect combination for you of interactions with people versus quiet working time?

Identify your talents. If you are not clear about your key talents, ask about what have you always been recognized for, perhaps particularly as a child? What do you do better than most other people? What skills do people seem to notice in you? What comes easy to you and what makes you joyful, happy, and smile, go further, work harder? I have learned a lot about this process from Talent+, an organization that offers particular interview questions for employers to identify a candidate's talents.

Now, on a piece of paper, your smartphone, or on your computer, write a list of words that best describes the different facets of your personality. This exercise is very important and will keep guiding you in the right direction. Ensure that this document is visible to you throughout your day, as it will remind you of who you are and what you do best.

You want to represent your brand well at all times by instilling a sense of well-being in your coworkers and customers, coupled with inspiration and excitement. This starts and ends with everything you do and say. People measure you because of your actions, but they critique you because of your non-actions. You gain value as both a person and a professional because you do the right thing—always.

Over the years, I have fine-tuned and shaped my own personal brand through developing a unique skill set, and by always remaining genuine and authentic. You will do this too as you grow both personally and professionally. For instance, you might not start out being a great public speaker, but this is something where the more you do it, the better you become.

For my brand, I always knew that I wanted to be a person of the world, someone who enjoys living and learning internationally. I like to engage with everyone on a professional level. I always believed in elegance. I tap-danced for my posture and because I am a fan of Fred Astaire. I love music and I played the trumpet very seriously when I was younger; when I was on stage, I had to perform. I realized that it's not just what comes out of your trumpet, but it's about your whole aura that you have when you go onstage; you need to capture the audience. This has translated into my role as a hotelier easily because, as people professionals, we want to capture the audience through who we are, no matter what "stage" we are on. For me, the moment you are in front of people, wherever that is, you have to perform at the highest level and you want to be at ease. I like to think I have an aura that makes people want to engage with me. I so enjoy being with people that I could do this job non-stop.

Of course, your personal brand will look different—everyone's will be unique and should be. This process will help you to define who you aspire to be, based on where you feel most comfortable.

REFLECT ON YOUR STORY TO STRENGTHEN YOUR FUTURE

I want you to focus on your story and your pathway to success, so that you can happily talk about your achievements with pride with colleagues, family, and friends. You are writing your own story today; every day you add a new page, and the more you do and contribute, the more you learn and the more successes you have, the better and more interesting your overall story becomes. Embrace everything, from failures to successes.

Keep a record of your key moments and things that made you better today than yesterday. I look at the key elements of my day—surprises, improvements, encounters with employees and guests—and see what made me a better person and professional today. It is a continuous story that helps me to improve consistently.

In doing this, you will see that all these parts add up and allow you to create a beautiful story of your personal and professional successes, strengthening your own personal brand. But don't gloss over your failures. These moments will stay with you for a long time. As painful as they are to relive and examine, eventually these experiences will help you to become a more competent professional. This may sound strange to say, but I do hope you have many failures, because without them you can't learn. They will make you stronger, more focused, and eventually a better leader, mentor, and a role model people aspire to emulate.

I think we have opportunities to learn about ourselves at each stage in our lives. If I opened the book of your life today and saw what stage you were in, I would never say, "Well, you should be at this stage right now, so why even bother. It's too late." No, it's never too late. Look at where you are right now and use it as a starting point rather than an end point. In principle #5 we'll talk about assessing your competencies and working on those—use that knowledge as a launch pad to help further where you are. If you've had a tough start in life or have had some disappointments—for instance, a bad manager where you couldn't get promoted, a hotel that might have closed, or even a natural disaster that shut down your workplace—and felt like it was a huge setback, use that experience as you move through life. You will be able to help deal with people in an empathetic way who have also experienced setbacks and disappointments.

Now that you are on the lookout for your brand, you will be better able to recognize what your talents and strengths are, and where you need to fine-tune your skills. You will remain weaker at other professional talents that are not your natural strong suits. For instance, a person who is not a numbers person may become competent at spreadsheets and filling out the right forms for the accountants but may never become the passionate financial expert that others may be. And those accountants may not be the best communicators in the world, though they may learn to write more effective emails and to present more effectively in meetings.

You might have heard the expression "success is never final." I would like you to think about your journey to success as one where every day you strengthen your foundation to go higher and grow stronger, more competent, and eventually achieve your desired professional destiny.

Your journey needs to be filled with joy, excitement, and celebrations, and therefore your hard work needs to be recognized—first by you. Don't expect that managers understand the importance of praise and motivation. Unfortunately, they may not, but that does not mean you should not have fun recognizing your successes. Plan a treat for yourself—a special night out with friends or a spa treatment, or choose an item of clothing that you have been wanting. Take a picture so you remember the occasion when you're looking back over pictures on your phone.

I often look back at my own story and how I have grown throughout my career. I did have mentors who assisted me tremendously, but in the end, it was my approach that led me to success. With the same focus, it will be the same for you. It is your own input, capabilities, strength, determination, willpower, as well as a little bit of luck, that will help you to achieve your destiny. Most important is that you are excited about your journey, and that your own story works for you and your loved ones and that you can have a fulfilled professional life that you can be proud of.

Your brand discovery will guide you naturally to where you would like to be. Please understand that the voyage to your desired success is long, yet exciting and fruitful. Every single step will help you to improve and make you the person you aspire to become. At every moment in your professional journey, you have a great opportunity to reflect and learn:

- What is your current role all about?
- Where you are strong and competent?
- Where you can add value to the team and everyone involved?
- Where do you lag behind?

Now is the moment where I ask you to come up with a short sentence that clearly communicates who you are. It should be simple and memorable and inspiring to you and your close friends. As an example, my own personal statement is "Touching hearts to inspire others to achieve their full potential."

> What is your personal statement?

Again, this is not just a slogan, but should clearly identify who you are, your strengths, what motivates you, what makes you stand-out personally and as a professional. It should contain part of your personality traits and your overall winning aura.

As we move on, we will look at your own vision and mission, then further, what competencies you may be lacking in order to move up the ladder and get to where you want to be. You can always update your statement at any point in your career, as it will change and shift depending on your job, supervisor, mentor, opportunities in the company, and especially if you change companies.

So take a deep breath, congratulate yourself on defining your brand, and let's do some more work on your path toward success.

CHAPTER EIGHT
PRINCIPLE #2:
DEFINE YOUR VISION AND MISSION

Your personal vision and mission will guide you to achieve what nobody else can do— achieving your own goals and dreams!
—Iwan Dietschi, Dr. Hotelier

Now that you have a better picture of your natural talents, strengths, motivations, and what makes you unique and happy, another key factor to achieving long-term success is understanding your professional ambitions and dream job, where you would like to be in the next twelve to eighteen months, three years, and then the next five to ten years from now. It all starts with identifying your personal vision and mission. I would like you to work on a personal vision and mission statement, which, in short, represents in a few phrases everything you would like to be, do, and experience in your career. It should incorporate your vision for what you would like to achieve professionally, while working on the present moment, representing your values, your purpose, and your goals.

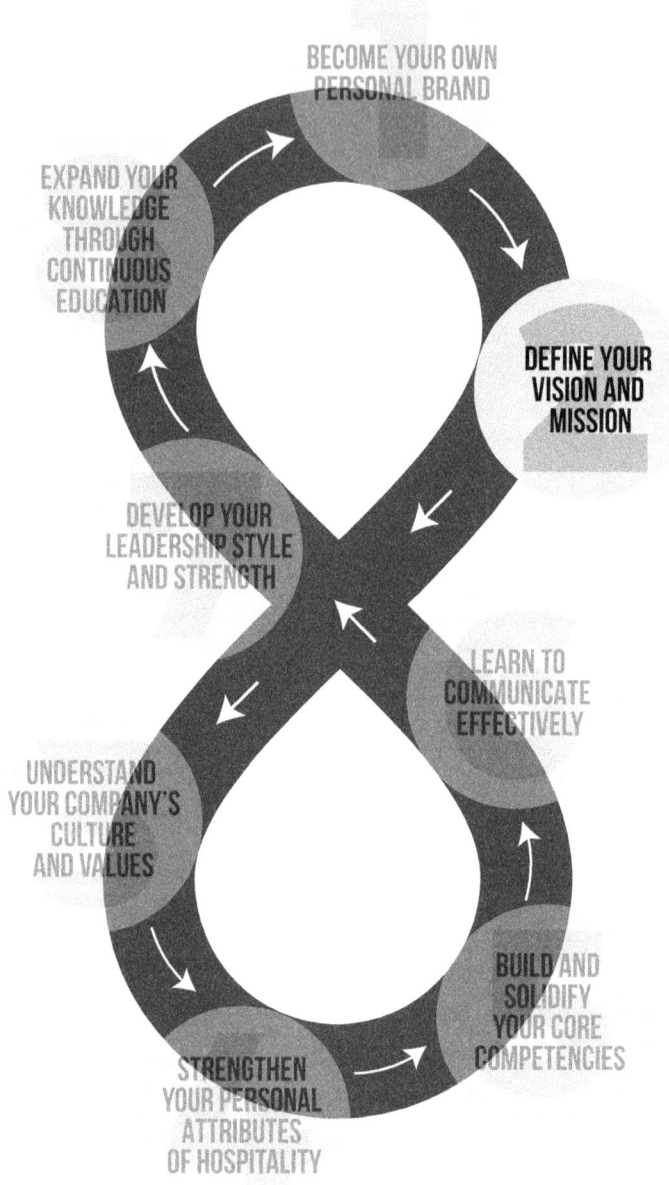

This aspect of Principle #2 for Excellence in the People Business is absolutely critical to ensure that you can clearly focus on your next steps with your vision in mind. Throughout my career, as well as during all my research, I learned that most leaders do not have a clear path to their own success. Most often, they happen to move up the ladder in their current company and achieve the next steps without properly planning, focusing, aligning, and seeking direction.

Do not get distracted by a great offer with more responsibilities and higher pay if it does not fit in your development plan, as you do not want to move up high to then potentially fall again because you did not have the necessary skills to sustain yourself. I am not saying that you should not take risks in taking on new opportunities, but please do weigh them properly (company, outlook, environment, growth opportunities, etc.). I would like you to avoid making the same mistakes and work on your own goals. You want to build your career on a solid platform, and the strength comes from building solid skills.

While your company itself may or may not have effective vision and mission statements, only a few executives I know have a clear personal statement for themselves. I strongly believe that executives should have a solid vision and mission statement for themselves as well. If executives are committed to leading with a corporate vision and mission and dedicate their professional lives to achieving those goals, it is expected (from my point of view) that they have their own statements guiding them. It's important for anyone to have a clear personal and professional

GPS, or compass in life, to focus on what is most important to them, and lead accordingly, enthusiastically, and with inspiration. Professionals should have short- and long-term goals and a means to incorporating them into their daily lives to guide themselves to achieve the highest possible satisfaction and best outcome for the people around them.

Today is the day when you are going to sit down and do what few other executives and leaders do: I want you to focus on your own direction for your future professional and personal success, based on your clear purpose, your long-term vision, and the steps needed to achieve your goals.

Every morning when you get up, I want you to be excited about the upcoming opportunity to go to work, to learn and grow and contribute to the company's and stakeholders' success. When you come back in the evening after work, I want you to be excited about the day you've had, about all the learning you did, and know that you made important contributions to your own growth, getting a step closer to your vision and dream job, and everyone you had the opportunity to work with, creating excellence. It's absolutely vital as well, even after a tough day, to be happy about the achievements you made, that you can fully focus on your family, your hobbies, and take care of yourself and all the important people in your life.

You have to focus on the good, learn from the bad, but know that you are always making contributions to your desired goal. A clear roadmap keeps you on track, allows you to be more relaxed about your failures and achievements, and helps you to create a more balanced life. You know what your next steps are and having a clear vision and mission helps you push your boundaries, keep the focus on what is most important, and prevents you from falling back into your comfort zone. I want you to build your career and life solidly with the right focus.

As part of your statement (which will be part of your daily life and visible at home, on your computer screen, on your mobile phone, or wherever you deem it necessary), take a look at and incorporate your long-term vision and goals. Then focus on how to achieve them by concentrating on smaller objectives—milestones—based on a yearly calendar, as an example. It is vital to plan for your future, and when it comes to thinking about your next job, you have to evaluate whether any new position fits with your goals and if this next step will allow you to improve your desired competencies as you fulfill the personal mission and vision you've set for yourself. Consider the key points I've highlighted below as you develop your own statement.

STEP 1:

Envision yourself in the top job you would like to achieve. Whether it is CEO of a small hotel company, general manager, vice president of an internationally renowned organization, or to have your own successful business—reach for the stars. Don't be shy. Don't hold back. I know you have dreams, so please be clear about them. Make your statement, first for yourself; then you can share it with your loved ones and anyone you deem necessary to know and understand your goal. I would like you to refer to an interesting and important book that helped me to further my development when I became a manager for the first time, Stephen Covey's *The 7 Habits of Highly Successful People*. In one of the chapters, he spoke about "Start with the End in Mind." This is absolutely critical, not only for your own vision and mission but also for any task you take on in your professional journey.

STEP 2:

Remind yourself of the personal values you wrote down in principle #1: Become Your Own Personal Brand and have them available to you as you go through this exercise. Furthermore, write down the purpose of your upcoming journey. What is your purpose in becoming what you are trying to achieve, and why is it important to you?

STEP 3:

Look at all the things you are good at, what you can contribute to others and any organization, and what makes you really happy with the skill sets you have. This is a critical base from where you need to build your competencies to reach what you want to achieve. It is like a company statement and should include for whom you want to do all this. Who can potentially benefit from your talents and future professional goal? Leaders of an organization have various stakeholders in mind when focusing on this part of the mission statement. For whom do we do it? Who will be the key beneficiaries?

STEP 4:

Now you can articulate your personal statement. Write at least two paragraphs, the first one focusing on your vision and the other, your way to achieve your vision, through a mission statement, incorporating your personal values and info from the above. Below I've included an example of a statement for you to better understand the overall purpose and outcome, as follows:

VISION:

> My goal is to become a president and CEO of an internationally renowned hotel or tourism company with a focus on creating excellence for all stakeholders and establishing the organization as a benchmark for the industry.

MISSION
(How to Get to Your Vision):

I will outline and follow my step-by-step improvement plan, growing through learning that is based on my purpose, talents, desires, and strengths. My aim is to have a balanced life with a clear focus and a way to touch people's hearts and minds through my work. I will contribute to the healthy growth of the business to exceed stakeholders' expectations.

I believe that this step of creating a personal vision and mission statement is an inspiring and exciting process. But the statement is only the beginning. A plan is only good if it is measurable, with a clear step-by-step approach, and achievable within a suitable and acceptable time frame. You will now have to work out clear goals within a particular time span. If your end goal is to become a general manager of a luxury hotel, you will need to have a clear comprehension of the path ahead. As mentioned previously, you need to understand where you currently stand professionally, which areas you have to improve your exposure in and gain competency, what your skills gap is, what kind of additional academic courses will contribute to your desired growth, and the leaders and mentors who will be able to assist you with your end goal in mind.

ENVISIONING YOUR DREAM JOB

I would like you to write down your dream job and the position you are aspiring to on a Post-it note, then place it in a strategic location in your apartment or house—for example on the mirror in the bathroom. There your dream job will be one of the last things you see before going to sleep at night, and it will be the first thing you see in the morning. Never let it out of your sight. This is not only to remember where you want to be, to dream big, and to ensure that you keep your focus, but to dedicate your day and learning to achieve your ideal outcome.

To achieve your fullest potential based on your brand, your vision and mission, you absolutely need to join the company that can support you in your quest to achieve your goals. The journey to success might take longer than you think, but just as you have a clear understanding of your next steps, you want to be part of an organization that can support you in your quest to achieve greatness. The next Principle, #3, looks at the value system and corporate culture of an organization. You need to be able to rely on solid support to move forward and to grow in all aspects of your career and therefore, matching your value system with your company will be extremely important.

CHAPTER NINE
PRINCIPLE #3: UNDERSTAND YOUR COMPANY'S CULTURE AND VALUES

Customers will never love a company until the employees love it first.
—*Simon Sinek, author of* Start with Why

A company's value system is designed to be embodied by everyone in the organization, therefore it is an important element to ensure you and the company achieve consistent success. For your own growth and development, I ask you to reflect strongly on this chapter to ensure that your value system is mirrored in the company's culture, and that leadership understands your talents and strength, and supports your growth ambitions. Corporate culture has become a favorite topic of mine because throughout my career, I've had the benefit of learning from excellent companies. When you focus on learning from the best, you can grow, benchmark, and implement strategies and actions in your own organization.

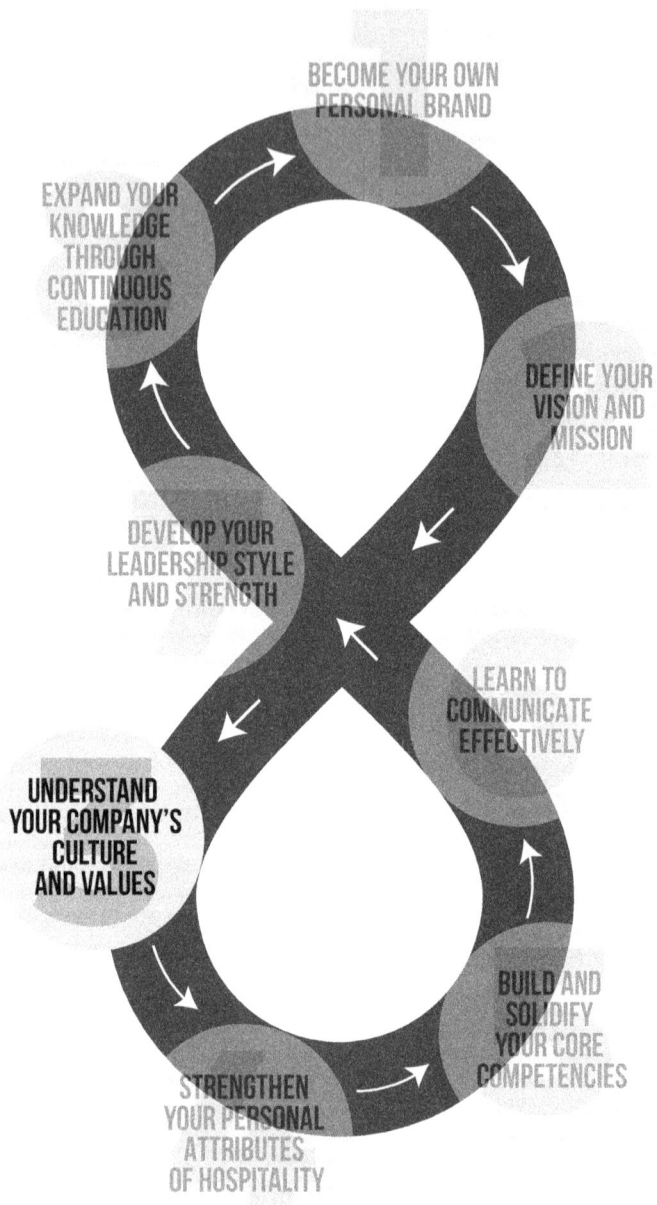

While corporate culture is not the only determinant of organizational success or failure, a positive culture can enable the smooth flow of information, and nurtures harmony among team members. Every leader, starting with the senior executives, has the duty and responsibility to strengthen the culture by their daily actions. Leaders in any industry must clearly model those values in their every action and communication. A corporate culture needs to be properly and consistently communicated with all, owned and lived by everyone in the organization, and based on a clear and easy-to-understand statement or slogans to achieve long-term company success.

WHAT IS CORPORATE CULTURE?

In an article on corporate culture, G. Jing[5] focused on four key elements that corporate culture needs to include: (a) A corporate culture has people-oriented management, where employees are highly valued and where communication and interaction with all employees and stakeholders from all different departments is a required basis for success; (b) shared values are the core element of corporate culture, which are consistent with the company's mission and vision and aligned with the personal values of its employees; (c) fostering of the corporate culture relies on all leaders and visible carriers; and (d) the criteria and the evaluation of any corporate culture is whether it can adapt to a competitive and ever-changing competitive market environment.

Employees' embracing the corporate culture is an important factor to consider for any company, because the constant reminder about why the organization exists and where the company is headed is required to have complete alignment from within. The work of Pinho, Rodrigues, and Dibb[6] emphasized the importance of creating an environment that fosters the cultural dimensions of atmosphere and connectedness, while limiting the constraining aspects of formalization, in order to enhance organizational performance. Additionally, Mark Schwartz[7] has found that firms need to ensure that within their broader corporate culture of shared values and beliefs, a strong ethical corporate culture also exists, rather than a weak culture.

Understanding those key attributes and communicating and teaching them to all employees in the organization are vital to create alignment, but it takes leadership and the top executives to lead the efforts on a daily basis. It's a critical aspect of the success of any organization, not just what is stated on the company's walls in frames that hang in the hallways, or what is written in the employee handbook, or what your leaders talk about during an interview or during orientation. Only *action* counts.

Credibility is strengthened by the guests and customers who embrace the organization based on their service and product delivery, consistency, and by the employees who move heaven and earth to achieve the highest possible guest satisfaction and build customer relationships that are real and based on mutual respect.

You have to challenge yourself to execute consistently based on the philosophy of the organization and its value system. For all leaders, you are watched by not only the employees, but by the guests and shareholders too. You have the duty and the responsibility to be an example at all times and in every situation. Do not disappoint your employees, your guests, or company. It takes a long time to create credibility of a brand, and it can be easily destroyed. As Warren Buffet said, "It takes twenty years to build a reputation and five minutes to ruin it. If you think about that, you'll do things different."

I challenge everyone to think about their own words, actions, and behaviors on a daily basis, with every single employee, guest, and how they represent the company through what they do or don't do. It takes a lot of self-reflection to understand that improvements can and probably do need to be made. My clear statement to you is that you have to identify with the company philosophy, rules, values, vision, and ensure that there is no compromise in aligning everyone in the organization. In many companies, not only in the hotel business, leaders make their own rules, but ask employees to do what the company states. My message to them is clear: *You are not credible; you will eventually lose good people, affect the business negatively, and slowly destroy the value of the company.*

A comprehensive corporate culture needs to communicate and embrace employees' growth opportunities and clearly highlight the importance of supporting anyone with the right desire, energy, competency, and proven track record to further learn and grow in their career.

With the corporate culture strategies, there are three core elements to keep in mind.

COMPANY VISION AND MISSION

Similar to a personal vision and mission, every company should have its own "compass." To achieve alignment among the critical stakeholders of the organization, a comprehensive and easy-to-understand and memorize vision and mission statement is absolutely vital to engage employees properly. This also helps to create joint understanding about the direction of the organization and to receive the needed buy-in from all the team members. A vision is the overall long-term goal for a company to aim for and focuses at the desired outcome and ideal future state for the company to achieve. The mission is a clear and easy-to-understand explanation of the organization's reason for existence.

With one or a few sentences, a mission statement explains how to achieve the vision. A strong and credible company direction needs to be at the base of the hotel's organizational success and represents a critical key to creating alignment between leadership and employees in the various departments. Furthermore, a vision and mission guides everyone in the hotel on how to operate the business on a daily basis.

As a team member, you should be part of writing or reviewing the mission statement yearly. It is critical that everyone comprehends and "owns" the required approach to achieve excellence together with the team. I have been involved in writing a lot of mission statements, as it is a core principle for employees to understand the overall desired business outcome, the approach, and the importance of the employees' involvement. A mission statement is your opportunity to define the company's goals, culture,

PRINCIPLE #3: UNDERSTAND YOUR COMPANY'S CULTURE AND VALUES

values, and norms for decision-making and should take into consideration three to four main points, as follows:

- What does your hotel (your department) do for your guests?

- What does the company, or your hotel, do for the employees?

- What does the organization (hotel) do for ownership and the community the hotel does business in?

I encourage you to search for some great examples of companies you really like and admire and find their "story" and mission and vision statements and see how they make them come alive through their products or their service excellence. We can always learn from other industries as well; therefore, do not limit yourself to just the hotel business.

VALUE SYSTEM

A clear set of values are the essence of a company's identity. I have always admired the simplicity of the values of our business as expressed by Mr. John Willard Marriott when he hailed, "People first," as a one of the hotel's core values. These are two distinctive and incredibly powerful words that explain everything about our business—the people business. Mr. Bill Marriott Jr. reminds all of us to take great care of the associates who will then take good care of the customer; then the customer will come back. This means we are all about making people feel good about themselves; and to be able to do this properly, it takes every single employee to be authentic in their behavior and in their interactions with other people. I talked about this earlier, that it is not only the most rewarding business, but a simple business, oftentimes made unnecessarily complicated. I know that you embrace the beauty of touching someone's heart and grow through giving experiences. This is the core of our business!

Understanding and living your company's values is essential for the organization's success. These values are the guiding principles to point you in the right direction and help you with making the right decisions for the company and all stakeholders.

CORE ALIGNMENT BY LEADERSHIP

A corporate culture dictates how employees and leaders treat one another, setting the tone and direction for how to conduct business on a daily basis. It is critical to emphasize the importance of aligning everyone on the corporate culture and that leaders need to own the philosophy and the values of the organization to achieve excellence in the team members. You as a leader need to reinforce the core values as part of the corporate culture. Employees will only follow you if you are true to the words through consistent actions. Every senior leader in the organization is challenged to support junior leaders and employees to achieve success in the various disciplines, especially when it comes to building competence throughout the organization.

At this stage of your career, you might not be a leader of your department yet, or you might still be in school. This topic will serve as an important guide throughout your career and when you grow to become a leader with responsibilities toward others.

Company leaders need to work on a way to consistently bring the core values alive throughout the company. There are many ways of doing this, benchmarking from the best. Again, the key point is to not only communicate but to bring it to life, every day.

Whatever your role or stage of your career, please remember that excellence does not have any shortcuts and that you are expected, like from anyone else in the organization, to make the vision come alive in every single interaction, communication, and action. Be part of the company's purpose, and become their most important advocate to achieve alignment and unmatched business success.

CHAPTER TEN
PRINCIPLE #4: STRENGTHEN YOUR PERSONAL ATTRIBUTES OF HOSPITALITY

> *It is one of the most beautiful compensations of life that no man can sincerely try to help another without helping himself.... Serve and thou shall be served.*
> —Ralph Waldo Emerson

With more than twenty-eight years in the luxury hotel industry, I wake up every morning with a smile on my face. This might sound strange to some, but it's the truth. I love to get up in the morning and prepare for work because I embrace every single day; a new day is a further opportunity to achieve greatness, to learn, and to grow.

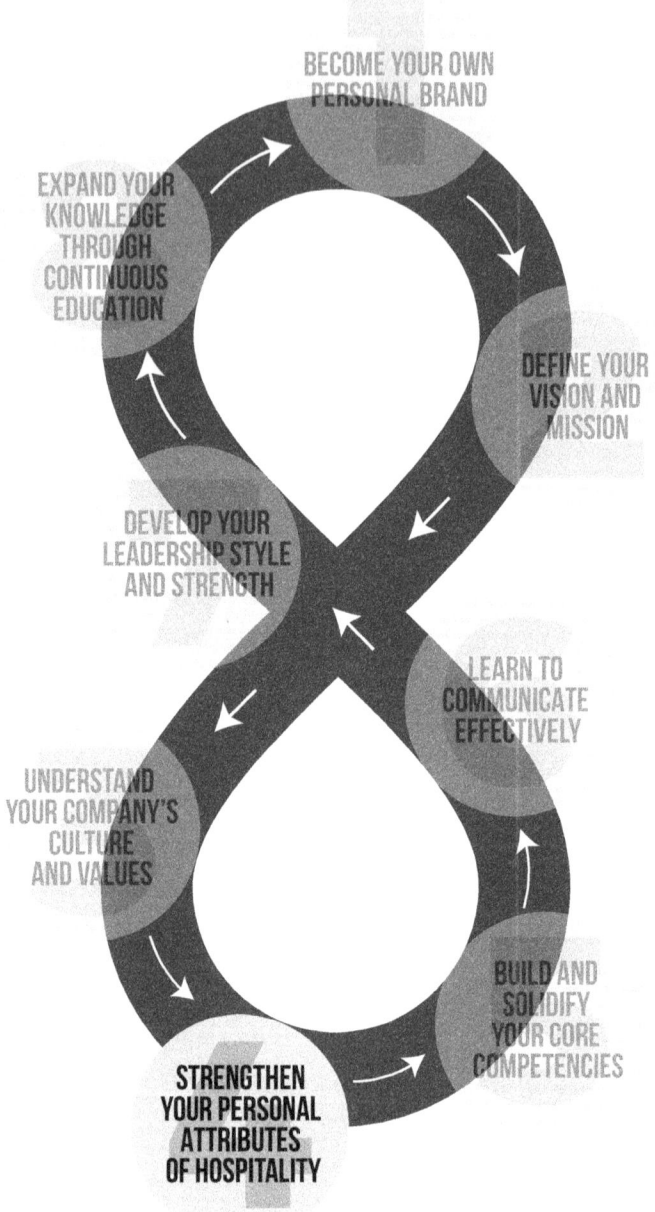

In our business, people always think it's about guests first. But I've learned and embraced the idea that hospitality, the People Business, is about employees first, then the guests and important stakeholders, and finally everyone who benefits from a healthy hotel operation, including the community. I wake up happy because it feels great to see my friends and colleagues and to create excellence together.

It is important that every day you look at improvement opportunities and fine-tune your ability to become the best that you can be in our business. I cannot state enough that you have to drive your own growth through competency-building on a technical level, regardless of your job function. Furthermore, there are additional key attributes of a people professional that are important to grow properly, to practice on a daily basis, and to incorporate into your daily lives to become a top professional.

BE A PERSON OF INTEGRITY

Integrity means being honest and having high moral and ethical principles. Integrity will help you in building a better relationship with your coworkers and everyone you deal with in your lifetime, as they know you are someone who can be trusted. You are measured throughout your life based on your integrity. You need to hold yourself consistently to the highest standards and never compromise!

BE HUMBLE

As we are in the people business, it's important to remember that we should never be arrogant when we're working with others. We must always be humble. Even when people are looking at us to be in charge, it's important to remember that we are always a supporting player. Success never comes from one individual, so whenever you get praise, give it to your people. Whenever you receive a complaint or witness a breakdown anywhere, you, as the future leader or executive, own it; don't blame others for shortfalls. The higher you go, the more exposure you receive. Never forget the team who makes you successful every single day. Highlight them, their efforts, their hard work, their commitment to you and your success. Learn and demonstrate that others are more important than you; therefore act and behave accordingly and make others feel good about themselves. You will earn not only their trust but their hearts and minds as well.

BE CHARISMATIC

The dictionary defines charisma as "compelling attractiveness," or "charm that can inspire devotion in others." I strongly believe that charisma can be learned and developed, as it is the result of excellent communication and interpersonal skills. As a person with charisma, you are an interesting person, and you want to show that you are intrigued by learning from other people as well.

Charismatic leaders have an amazing ability to positively influence others. Optimism is a key strength of a charismatic person and leader. You can turn negatives into positives and look at the bright side of issues and concerns. Your messages need to end on a positive note and in a way that your audience is captured, inspired, and excited to not only listen but to execute on any directives with enthusiasm.

To be charismatic, you want to tell a credible story that people can understand and identify with clearly. Credibility is absolutely vital to building strong followers and to capturing their hearts and minds. I learned this skill over the years, and most importantly, I was able to better articulate the message, a shared vision, even an ideology that is important to the success of so many.

Charismatic leaders are very persuasive. They use effective rhetorical strategies and verbal and nonverbal clues, which are critical, and they balance them well when it comes to the delivery of the message, always understanding who their audience is.

A charismatic leader is empathetic and not egotistical. It's true that charismatic people are confident, or at least they project confidence. You will gain that confidence as you grow as a person and a leader in your business by developing your own approach to personal and professional excellence. A confident leader has the ability to communicate in all sorts of situations, whether it be in a one-on-one meeting or at a large sales conference of five hundred people. A true leader has a great ability to make others feel good about themselves.

BE DIPLOMATIC AND A BRAND AMBASSADOR

It is imperative that as you represent the brand of your business, you are diplomatic when speaking with guests and always have the best outcome for the guest in mind. As a professional, you always want to make the guest feel comfortable. Everything should revolve around the guest. The customer should be the center of attention and focus—make them feel taken care of at any moment in time so that they leave the conversation or discussion with a positive personal feeling, as well as a positive feeling about you, the hotel, and the brand. The customer will appreciate your professionalism and viewpoints if given in an appropriate, positive, engaging way. Keep your personal opinions, political viewpoints, and sensitive topics and arguments to yourself when communicating with business partners, guests, and various stakeholders. It is critical that you know your audience. Understand to whom you speak with and always ensure that you are sensitive to the discussion, the topic at hand, and empathize with the person you engage with. You are a top professional and need to know how to behave, even if you do not like the subject matter and do not agree with all the viewpoints before you.

As a hotelier and people professional, you need to be at ease to speak with anyone at any time and to engage in a conversation to add value to the other person. It is a great way to improve your know-how and sets you apart from the rest. Do not forget, if you add value to others, they will not forget about you, and they will come back for more.

BE CURIOUS

Curiosity is about being interested not only in what motivates and drives you but in everything that has to do with your profession, your goals, your aim in your job, and the people and guests around you. You need to find ways to remain on the lookout for new elements that can bring you to the next level. Your passion and drive will lead you to new heights, but know that it is clearly up to you to make that difference for yourself. Our business is filled with information. Your curiosity and interest in personal and professional knowledge will allow you to learn in any situation, at any time, anywhere.

Curiosity helps you find answers to "why," and then you will learn, improve, and ask "why" again. Inventions all have happened because of curiosity, because of always wanting to improve and find new ways, because of a strong will to make a difference, to change, and to create something new and better. Curiosity leads to knowledge and expertise and will help to improve products, services, and people's understanding and growth.

In my experience, the world in our profession is open to us, and I took the chance to be flexible and focus on the next opportunity. This made me stronger and more competent. A people professional understands different cultures, is eager to see the world and learn from others, and takes the time to plan their career wisely, if possible, to become a citizen of the world. Again, I had opportunities because I was looking for them, and my drive to travel and grow throughout various continents allowed me to be the "complete hotelier" I am today. I talked about the countries I have visited and worked in, but I will not talk about all the wonderful people I met, as it is an honor, a privilege, and a commitment to these people not to speak about various encounters. A top professional conducts himself or herself with discretion—it should be part of who you are. Most important is to focus on all of these experiences and understand how to combine them to make you a better professional, and most crucial, discretion is key.

BE PATIENT

Patience means the ability to accept or tolerate a delay, problems, or suffering without becoming annoyed or anxious. I strongly believe patience is critical to success in life, particularly in the business world. You have to learn to accept that not everything always goes according to plan and that your circle of influence is somewhat limited. Where you can make a difference, you will need to show your competence, your leadership, and your patience as you need to teach and communicate in a productive, uplifting, and oftentimes repetitive way. Losing your temper will have a long-lasting and sometimes negative impact on everyone around you.

Patience can be learned, and it will help you to have a more happy life. Having patience means being calm when facing an obstacle or a frustrating situation. A patient person demonstrates tranquility and mastery of a situation, will be able to think properly and constructively, and won't be distracted by annoyances. Patience will help you to remain positive and to be optimistic. You will learn that decision-making requires a clear head, constructive discussions, professionalism, and the ability to weigh various points. Believe me, you will have ample time to practice, improve, and make patience an important attribute during the course of your career.

BE AUTHENTIC

I speak about authentic leadership in more detail later, but I would like to reemphasize how important it is to be authentic, to let people know and feel who you are, as only true leaders understand the importance of authenticity and value. Your goal as a leader is to guide, inspire, and support your employees at all times, creating the desire in them to work harder toward common goals. A true leader is someone people trust. Period. An authentic leader always speaks the truth, communicates clearly and effectively, acts ethically, is transparent, approachable, and has an unwavering commitment to the growth and well-being of her or his employees.

Authentic leaders demonstrate strong self-discipline with a focus on the most important aspects of the job. A true leader always says what he or she means and does what he or she says they will do, and they consistently "walk the talk," creating an example for others to follow.

CHAPTER ELEVEN
PRINCIPLE #5:
BUILD AND SOLIDIFY YOUR CORE COMPETENCIES

Do what you can, where you are, with what you have.
—Theodore Roosevelt

This principle looks at the need to further your own core competencies consistently, with a clear plan to achieve your professional goals. Wherever you are in your career, look at what you need to do to become the best at your current job, and prepare yourself for future growth and higher positions.

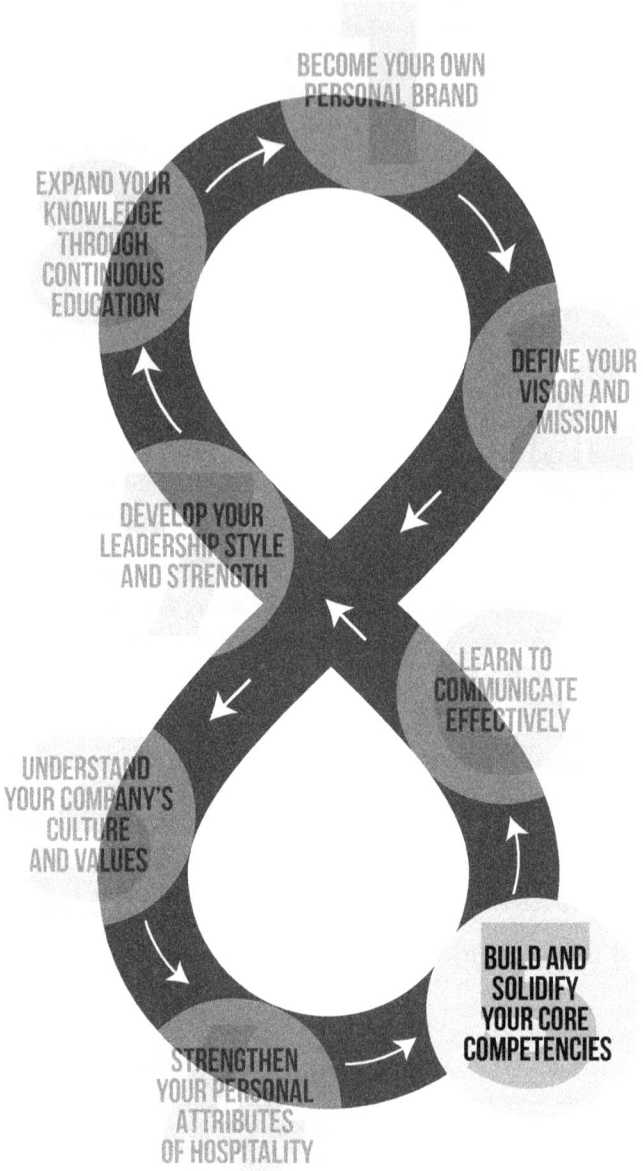

As I stated before, no matter what position you have currently, you will need to become a master at your task. It is vital to your growth to understand your shortfalls and to follow an improvement plan to achieve your next steps. You have to spend time on developing your own strategy for growth, based on your current role, strengths, shortcomings, your competency gap, and your own vision and mission. Although you will require the support and inspiration from your immediate leadership and the company in your growth strategy, it is *you* who will drive your success. Every single day you can learn and improve and you will naturally assist others, the department or the division to take positive steps to reach the next level. Please, never wait to be asked. You should always remain proactive and keep your eyes on the ultimate prize.

Customers are able to send comments about their guest experiences with ease these days through social media on sites like TripAdvisor, Twitter, and Instagram. If you are in a visible and perhaps front-of-house position, it is ideal to have the natural desire and drive to be public and visible with your name on guest posts as often as possible. Customers should recognize who you are, the effort you make, and most importantly, how professional you are in creating unmatched experiences alone or together with your peers.

By working on your competencies, you will raise your profile not only with your guests, but with your managers, leaders, colleagues, and the executive team. Here are some areas where it's important to concentrate your focus as taking a larger role in your career:

time management, making the most of meetings, presentation skills, creative thinking, and critical thinking.

TIME MANAGEMENT

One of the most important skills to learn is the art of planning and organizing your time. As your job requires that you must plan your day weeks out or even months in advance, as a future leader in the luxury hotel industry, or in any people profession, you need to demonstrate this skill to everyone around you. It's important to know how to plan your time wisely to have more productive days and not to waste time.

Good time management enables you to work smarter—not harder—so that you get more done in less time, even when time is tight and pressures are high. Failing to manage your time will hurt your overall effectiveness, causing stress and frustration.

I've learned this lesson the hard way throughout my career, most recently during the time I worked on my executive MBA and then my doctorate. In my experience, the best way to plan your week is on the Friday prior to the coming week. Take out your calendar and write down all your key dates, meetings, calls, and everything that's important to you. For instance, when I was working on my doctorate, during a busy workweek, I tried to schedule two evenings (Tuesdays and Thursdays) to work on my assignments and my dissertation. I tried to reserve the time from 7:30 p.m. until 11:00 p.m. Then I planned five hours each Saturday and

Sunday to complete outstanding schoolwork or further advance with my research.

Working and studying is just one example, but as a busy professional, I clearly needed to know when I had the time to do the important tasks, when I had time for meetings and follow-ups, when I could organize my one-on-one meetings with my other GMs or key leaders, and when I had time for the gym. (Never forget to schedule your activities, as you need to keep your work-study-life balance at all times. Please remind yourself to sleep enough as well. Time management will help you to achieve this goal.)

With time management also comes prioritizing your tasks, communicating to your team if you need the time to work quietly, and delegating items on your list if possible so that you can balance everything. Set automatic reminders on your phone so that you don't forget that you should be on a phone call or if you should be leaving for a meeting.

You must conquer your toughest, most uncomfortable task first thing in the morning so it doesn't hang over your head for the rest of the day and interfere with your ability to concentrate on your other tasks. Also, turn off emails, your web browser if you can, and all but essential phone calls while you are working on an essential task.

I encourage you to find the best way to manage time for yourself. Everyone is different, and no one program is a good fit for all. Great leaders understand their schedule, know how to plan to make them successful, and clearly demonstrate competency in managing their time properly, effectively, and efficiently.

MAKING THE MOST OUT OF MEETINGS

Meetings are important for many reasons: to get people on board with a situation, to get status updates, to come up with ideas as a team, to further strengthen relationships, etc. To create alignment, trust, and the needed buy-in of the employees and all parties involved when you communicate in a meeting, you as a leader or future leader have to create that openness among the team members to engage in the conversation and in the tasks that affect your own job, or it will have an impact on employees or guests. A solid company and a great leader always leave room for anyone to make comments, suggestions, and to further improve the process or the desired outcome. An open approach to communication allows a company to tap into the innovative spirit of the employees and creates that inspiration among everyone involved to participate in a way to further improve overall outcome for all stakeholders.

Whenever you meet with others in a formal or even an informal setting during work time, you are spending company money for everyone to come together. Meetings can become boring, irrelevant, and uninspiring, and in the end you leave without having received any important information. This can be prevented by building the important skill of knowing how to organize a meeting. Below I highlight a few critical aspects for you to learn, further improve, and think about when organizing meetings:

- Prepare all aspects of the meeting, clearly communicating the purpose to others in advance so everyone is ready.

- Send out a meeting outline to everyone with the required time and duration of the meeting and its purpose.

- Be on time to host your meeting. This means that you should be at least ten minutes early, as you want to greet everyone. You can expect everyone else to be five minutes early as well. It shows discipline, focus, commitment, and is polite.

- Start the meeting with something encouraging or inspiring to get the full attention of your employees or other leaders.

- Be a solid and careful listener, as you want to demonstrate true leadership and to ensure that everyone has a voice and gets respect through personal involvement into any discussion.

- Encourage everyone to participate. This is not always easy, but if you follow the points above, you will create an environment where people are focused, excited, and where they feel safe and can share their opinion.

- Take notes or have someone take notes on your behalf, and ensure they get communicated to all parties involved after the meeting, as soon as possible.

- Always end the meeting by thanking the participants. This will create a stronger bond with the attendees, strengthening your relationship with them and inspiring them to "go out there now and create." Encourage them to take immediate action on issues and items discussed.

You, as the leader or aspiring leader, want to keep following up on the assignments and allow the team members to ask you questions or for input at any time.

To become effective in conducting meetings, you'll need to practice and learn from the best. There are many opportunities for you to improve your skills by listening, taking notes, observing, and learning from both the good and the bad. Yes, unfortunately, many leaders and managers do not know how to organize and conduct a meeting properly and professionally and therefore waste people's time and company money. Never forget that when you meet others in a formal setting, those managers or employees are taken away from their normal duties, where they should be with employees and guests to further improve overall products and services. Your responsibility during a meeting needs to be clear and more important than whatever other duties the meeting participants have. When you call a meeting, you are taking the participants' time, so make it productive, interesting, inspiring, and meaningful, adding value to the company and all stakeholders.

PRESENTATION SKILLS

How does it make you feel when you know that you have to talk in front of others—do you feel confident that you can speak knowledgably about a subject and engage your audience, or do you fear that you might stumble over your words, pale, sweaty, losing where you are in your notes, while your audience yawns and checks their phones?

My late father was a fantastic presenter. When I was young, I used to watch him practice his speeches—he was still practicing, even though he was already experienced at giving them. He taught me that when I wrote a presentation, it was important to highlight key words and phrases to get my message across. I used to practice my speeches over and over again in front of the mirror, and then later presented my speech to my father, who would give me feedback on what I could improve. During hotel school, certain courses were available to fine-tune this important skill, which allowed every student to receive critical feedback.

The first presentation I gave at work was when I was a young assistant manager. I was tasked with presenting ideas from a recent business book in front of sixty leaders, mostly senior employees of the big hotel where I worked. I was nervous for days beforehand.

I started to prepare as much as I could, first by reading the book, highlighting what seemed to be the important points, and trying to memorize the key elements of the topic. I wrote small cheat sheets to prepare, and I was practicing as my father had taught me in front of the mirror, even recording sequences of the speech to review. But on the day of the presentation, when I was standing in front of the audience, everyone looking at me made me uncomfortable.

Just when my nerves threatened to overwhelm me and ruin my presentation, I remembered back to when I was playing a trumpet solo in front of an audience and how great it had felt then to engage with my audience back when I had an instrument.

Why was this so much harder? As I went through more of my presentation, I began to feel more comfortable, but I had a bad feeling afterward, as I was not as relaxed as I had wanted to be.

What was the big lesson? You can become good at anything by practicing, and again, practicing. I was not nervous as a musician because I practiced playing trumpet every day. I'd done it so much, I knew my performance was solid. I was passionate about performing, and I wanted everyone to hear my music. I was confident, and I knew I would get applause at the end.

Well, you want to have the same feeling when you make a presentation in front of people. It's like going onstage because you are the "act," and you want your audience to be excited and inspired. Most importantly, an opportunity to speak and talk in front of others gives you momentum, because it puts you front and center, where you can get noticed and you can fine-tune your own brand with what you want to get noticed for.

This is a great opportunity to differentiate yourself from others, because we all know there are other managers who almost bore you with their presentations. Nothing can be worse than sitting in a business meeting where your executives speak and do a less-than-inspiring job. You almost begin to wonder how they got to their high position if they are not effective presenters. Yes, not everyone is a brilliant performer or presenter, but the higher you go in the hierarchy, the better you have to become at it. It is like your business card, and most of these people not only represent themselves and the company, but you as well, and every employee of your organization.

Here are some tips that helped me to succeed.

TO PREPARE:

- Know your topic well.
- Learn about your audience and their reason for listening to you.
- Think about the message you want to deliver.
- If you do a PowerPoint presentation, keep the information on the slides to the key topics only, and please, never read off a slide.
- Outline the first phrase of each new subject on a piece of paper (a cheat sheet) to get you started after each paragraph and topic.
- Ensure that you capture the audience with something light in tone or with a statement that touches their hearts and minds.
- Know your sequences well.
- First, practice your presentation in front of a mirror and then record the entire speech. I want you to look at yourself, the words you use, how you articulate them, and then your overall presentation. Are you confident? Do you stand straight? Do you smile? Are you just talking, or are you capturing your audience with words, gestures, tone, pauses, reflections, jokes, and questions?
- Pay attention to your overall look and manner. You should be well dressed because you are on stage, and you should come across as happy and focused, not stressed and anxious.

SHORTLY BEFORE THE PRESENTATION:

- Make sure you go to the bathroom and look at yourself in the mirror; look at your teeth, and confirm that your appearance is appropriate to conquer the audience. Don't forget what you and your brand are.
- Practice a joke or something you can throw in to lighten everyone up.
- Ensure that you have a glass of water or a bottle of water next to the podium or somewhere within reach.

DURING YOUR PRESENTATION:

Once you enter the stage, without arrogance, stand firm, look at the audience, smile, take a deep breath, and start with a phrase to welcome everyone and make them either smile or think. Go through the presentation as you have practiced, and always keep eye contact with the audience. If you feel uncomfortable, imagine that everyone in the audience has little piglet ears. This will help make you less nervous and will put a smile on your face.

Don't walk around the stage—this makes people nervous. Stand firm. Yes, you can move if you want to engage the audience, but only to keep them focused and not because you can't keep still.

If you lose track of your speech, share the joke you practiced earlier. This will give you time to look at your paper and find a new entry into your presentation.

Thank the audience at the end, and always give them something to think about or reflect upon. Not your entire speech, but a particular question, anecdote, or a slogan that completes your presentation.

Walk away with confidence, look at the audience, smile, and even if you feel that you made mistakes, keep your posture upright, and show pride, elegance, confidence, and competence.

A speech can be extremely powerful and captivating with (a) the right content, (b) the repetition of the key words and phrases, and (c) the tonality and effective presentation skills of the content onstage or wherever you present it. Through practicing, you will gain that confidence required to create a successful outcome and to become the best that you can be. These days you have more opportunities than ever because you can learn through the internet from skilled presenters on TED Talks and in other formats to see the most successful speakers.

DEVELOP YOUR CREATIVE THINKING SKILLS

Improving your creative thinking can make a big difference in your career. In general, being someone with a rigid thinking approach in one domain is a good predictor you will be inflexible with your thoughts in other areas or domains. I strongly believe your drive and creativity will create potential opportunities that will lead you to the appropriate resources available to master your thoughts, learn, grow, and improve your creativity.

A Harvard Business School professor, Teresa M. Amabile, mentioned that creativity is not enough in business to achieve success. To be creative in any environment, but particularly in business, an idea must also be appropriate, useful, and actionable. Any idea that gets implemented has to make business sense. You have to evaluate if it is in accordance with the strategy and if it is based on the purpose statement of your department, operation, and hotel.

Company executives are always asking for more innovations, as any product or service needs to evolve. I want you to look back at the innovative ideas, processes, or products you've implemented so far in your career. I've seen creativity thrive through giving employees the power to decide, to take action, and to constantly create based on employees' professional input and know-how.

A certain amount of autonomy, or freedom, to make decisions will eventually spur creativity, potentially resulting in innovative employees. A critical aspect is to create a work environment where employees are encouraged to be part of the process to improve products and service delivery. Every department should build smaller teams to analyze customer feedback, input from employees, and keep an eye on the competition and new trends. This team can have a tremendous impact and work with the support of leadership on new products or fine-tuning service components. These team members should be handpicked not only by the leader but by peers as well. Many employees are eager and excited to contribute to a better work environment and to create the products of tomorrow.

You might have experienced such a team and efforts like this before, but if not, I urge you to think about it, as the best ideas usually come from your own team members. It will help to increase their motivation to drive results, support others, and to develop their innovation, creativity, and leadership skills. Creating new products takes drive and commitment, as well as ability, guidance, support, and the freedom to make decisions.

Innovation in our business can be incremental, improving, changing, or completely revolutionizing a process, service, or product delivery. Creative or innovative thinking needs to be deeply rooted in the company culture and encouraged throughout the organization. Creativity means failing from time to time as well, but that should not deter you or anyone from continuing to try out new ideas. The more you do it, the better you will become at it.

Creativity needs space, motivation, inspiration, and time, and sometimes even money. Empowerment needs to be a key focus in any company, and you as a leader or future leader need to demonstrate what that means, and in particular, how it can, should, and does affect employee and guest satisfaction, team spirit, and innovation. It also creates a work environment of mutual support and trust, where everyone is encouraged to contribute to the overall success of the department and hotel.

I want you to have the courage to think differently and to speak up. Not every idea will be brilliant, but the fact that you have spoken up and communicated your viewpoint to others will help to start a healthy discussion about a particular topic.

I strongly believe that successful, creative people learn most from feedback. They weigh important comments and are never discouraged to take that feedback and assess their content to further build on a better way or solution and act accordingly.

As a creative thinker, you want to look at a process, product, or service that was inspired by someone else or from another industry, then try to adapt and implement it into your own area or operation. This process allows you to learn everything you need to know about it, remodel it, then transform it to your own area. It allows you to learn and grow and to eventually make an impact on your own hotel. Do not be shy to learn from others, as we are no magicians.

Creative thinkers use processes and methods that can be learned. For instance, I have studied various companies, in technology and in retail. Alibaba and its founder, Jack Ma, transformed the digital space and the way many people shop nowadays. It was fascinating to observe how Alibaba created product after product, invented the 11/11 singles' shopping day, and made the task of shopping much easier and more exciting through its various applications and the products it made easily available from around the world. In retail, Nordstrom, a US company, has always been at the forefront of customer service. The salesperson can ring up your purchase from anywhere in the store using mobile checkout devices. Employees are directed and empowered to use their best judgment to make the customer happy, so they will continue to come back for more. Another example of innovative thinking is Marriott International, with the biggest loyalty program in the industry, utilizing mobile technology to enhance experiences. Mobile check-in, mobile requests, and mobile key room access are only a few. Technology in many aspects will become more important for guests. There are so many great examples from incredible companies around the world, and I encourage you to do your own research to be at the forefront of the ever-changing technological and other innovations and to spur your own creative mind.

BECOME A LOGICAL, CRITICAL THINKER

Nowadays, we all get flooded with information through the news, social media feeds, people who share their stories, experiences, and beliefs, and all kinds of private messaging. It is often difficult to be sure of the core facts or the real meaning behind an event, opinion, or problem. I urge you to not simply accept what is presented in front of you. An intelligent person, someone who always seeks to understand the full picture, thinks logically and critically. This shows that you do more than simply acccpt the status quo or the presented facts—you seek a deeper understanding to your own satisfaction. This ability enables you to go into almost any situation and to figure out the nature of whatever is happening, allowing you to make better, more sound decisions.

Unfortunately, critical thinking is a competency that has gotten lost. Too many people are too easily satisfied with answers and therefore are more easily influenced. You, as a leader or future leader, need to improve this skill by always asking questions. I learned to find the underlying cause of a situation by never being satisfied with an answer, which then allows me to ask further questions. Asking WHY, WHY, WHY—as many times as you need—is absolutely critical. I want you to become your own thinker, to acquire your own logical approach to questions or statements, or so-called facts. You have to practice this skill like any other. You will be surprised how many doors or windows it will open for you. I have questions every day, and I learned to go deeper to be sure I can get to the truth about something of importance to me.

I learned a long time ago that a sign of intelligence is asking the right question and then asking a question again. I want you to become extremely knowledgeable and independent in your thinking process, as it will improve your overall understanding, and with knowledge you will find the right answers. As I've said, you always learn more from your mistakes than from successes. I would like you to become the best that you can be by understanding that you can be wrong but then quickly learn from it, improve, and further solidify your competencies.

Critical thinking refers to higher-order thinking that questions assumptions and is described as "thinking about thinking." Critical thinking has helped me to evaluate facts, to weigh opinions, and to ensure that I have my own viewpoints on matters. We all are too quick to judge on issues, and our thinking behind a statement is oftentimes biased, the information we are judging incomplete and potentially distorted. To be the best you can be, you have to be able to rely on the quality of your thoughts; your life, your job, your responsibility as a human being and a top professional depend on it. Critical analysis is a skill you need to improve to avoid just accepting statements or potential solutions presented to you without thought.

As a critical thinker, you raise questions that are important to any issue or problem, clearly understanding the subject matter, and can describe and communicate precisely. Furthermore, your ability to think logically allows you to gather and assess key information relevant to the subject matter and interpret it effectively. It is vital to arrive at a solid and well-reasoned conclusion and solution, testing the outcome against your own and other relevant standards. Learn to think with a clear and open mind, with an ability to recognize and assess the assumptions and the potential consequences. Become an expert communicator to lead the way to effectively focus on sustainable solutions to potentially complex issues. In a world where information and knowledge is the key to personal and professional growth, and in a certain way, your own fulfillment and the right state of mind, curiosity, and critical thinking can be useful tools to helping you grow.

I've learned so much simply by asking "why" several times in order to get a broader viewpoint. Never take anything for granted, but do not waste your time to further elaborate on a topic that is not relevant to you, your colleagues, your business, and takes you away from more important things to do.

We are surrounded by information, data, and the world of knowledge through media and the internet with the assistance of the many devices we possess. You need to decide what information is relevant and what can assist you in your quest to improve your professionalism and ability to perform your job at the highest level. Furthermore, what information is actually true. An important lesson is to never talk or comment on social media about a topic that you have not verified. Don't speak about it with others either. Always think about the damage an ill-informed remark or take on a current event can do to your professional and personal brand.

I am oftentimes amazed by how educated people simply accept information presented to them without taking the time to conduct due diligence to verify facts. I want you to become a savvy consumer of news and information and assess the sources to find out what is truly relevant, correct, and can add value to your life and career and to the important people around you. I realize that it is not always easy to come to the right conclusion, but I encourage you to fine-tune this skill and ask important questions, like "why?" I would like you to use a similar drive when you look at gaining overall knowledge about topics of particular interest to you.

During meetings and conversations, speak up if you have questions or require additional information. When you disagree or you believe that there is more to a topic, voice your concern or add your input in an open but respectful way. You want to challenge people in a courteous way to help you get to the bottom of something that is important to you, that you deem necessary to do your job properly, or that helps everyone to grow.

Be empathetic and conscious of what you say and how you say it to further strengthen your brand.

With time, you will understand which sources are credible and which content is important to you and is based on facts.

CHAPTER TWELVE
PRINCIPLE #6: LEARN TO COMMUNICATE EFFECTIVELY

Since in order to speak, one must first listen, learn to speak by listening.
—*Rumi*

It is vital in the hotel business to communicate effectively—with both our guests and fellow staff members. Mix-ups anywhere along the line can have consequences that can negatively affect our business: from dissatisfied employees, garnering bad reviews on social media, to orders that didn't get placed, deliveries that didn't get made, reservations that didn't go through. When things go wrong and feelings get hurt, business is on the line. Clear and effective communication is crucial to saving the day, to learn and grow properly, and to build needed trust and stability within a team.

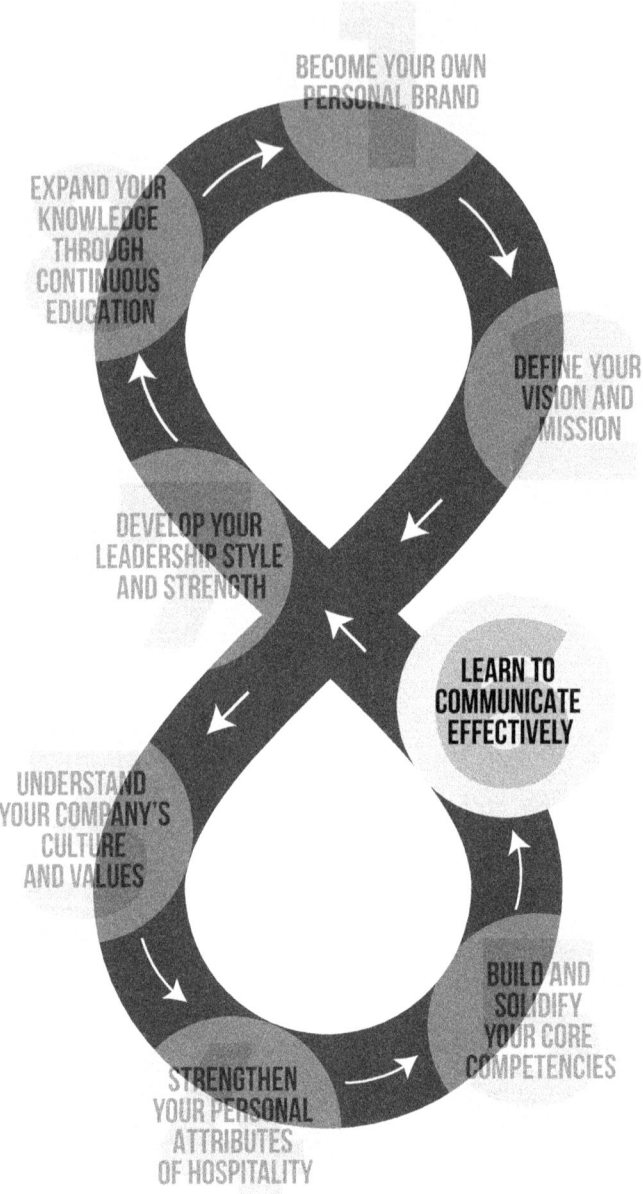

PRINCIPLE #6: LEARN TO COMMUNICATE EFFECTIVELY

Communication requires you to exchange verbal and nonverbal messages as part of a two-way process. It is absolutely critical that the message that gets to the other party is clear and accepted in the way it was meant to be communicated. Your nonverbal cues—your posture, your smile, your gestures—should be in alignment with your words and your tone, how you say what needs to be said, and when you deliver your message. Communication requires clear alignment and should not leave any space for further interpretation.

It's not always easy to find the right tone at all times. I call it the "tonality art," as you are playing your voice like an instrument. Knowing how to use your voice and tones to emphasize and strengthen your message is a skill to be practiced, so instead of sounding like a harassed and put-out employee, you sound like a calming port in a storm, one who can solve all the problems of the person who is experiencing a maelstrom.

Another example of using tone, illustrated earlier, is if you are giving a presentation and you are trying to highlight a particular word or key words, you then speak more loudly and slow down the speed to clearly pronounce those words. Another helpful tip is to take a breath, or breaks, between phrases or paragraphs, to focus the audience, and to make the entire discussion or points more interesting and captivating. I learned that silence can be an incredible energizer for the audience, as they become more focused on your words and overall body language. This space—this silence—in between the words captures the attention of your listeners and allows them to better receive your message.

I want you to look for various signs that are key to improving your overall communication style and approach. Nonverbal cues are gestures, eye contact, behavior, physical appearance, to name a few. This requires you to learn about other cultures. Because our cultures differ from one another, your gestures and behavior might mean something entirely different to the other person from what it means to you. This also requires your openness to learn from different people with diverse backgrounds. In general, we all seem to judge people too fast. This is especially important to remember for those of us in the hotel and tourism sector, where we are privileged to engage and host guests from all around the world.

It's important not to assess a person prematurely and without having adequate information about them. Many people are tempted to judge others, but as a professional you have to be extremely careful. One way to learn to not do this is to avoid speaking before thinking, which means that you should always weigh your words before you act. A professional in any business has to learn from potential consequences prior to speaking or acting in a judgmental way. You cannot take back words or retrieve your emails once you send them out.

Every culture has different types of behavior that might be unique to their people when it comes to norms. It could be around physical closeness, what will be tolerated as far as manners are concerned, what is considered acceptable, and what is expected. You as a top professional in the people business need to understand what is appropriate and what might make others uncomfortable. For example, people might be offended or uncomfortable when their immediate space is not kept. Some people might find it offensive if you place a hand on them, whereas you might think you are being comforting.

Spend time learning about what is acceptable and what is not to other cultures. There are excellent guidebooks and training videos out there for business travelers. It's so important to remember how words are just a small portion of communication and often are less important than your actions and the way you bring a message to the recipient.

WRITTEN COMMUNICATION

I would like to emphasize the importance of the written communication in our daily lives, be it personal or professional. This form of communication is present everywhere through email, text messaging, online chats, letters, memos, guest welcome cards, or simply birthday wishes. You want to become very effective in your written communication to ensure that the receiver clearly understands the content and "hears" the message in a polite and pleasing tone. Yes, tone of voice, even with the written word, is often felt. Therefore, it is paramount that you take time to ensure the tone of your writing matches the spirit of your message—be it casual or professional.

Everything you write reflects on you, your personal brand, and the company you represent. Your communication becomes your "business card." As with so many other skills, every day you have the chance to improve, benchmark, and ensure that everything you write is a reflection of what one would expect from a people professional.

There are many parallels to verbal communication and both go hand-in-hand. As a best practice, you want to read through everything you write at least once and sometimes several times before you release it. You want to look closely at the overall clarity of the content, the structure and grammar, the tone, and how well the writing fits its intended purpose. Again, please make sure you re-read first, rather than pushing that "send" button too early. You might regret it!

On the flip side, a well-written document or text can enhance your overall reputation and image, not only in the business world but also among your friends and family.

Please fine-tune your handwriting as well. It's almost a lost art but the personal, handwritten note can capture the reader in a very positive way—or then irritate if it is not easily legible. A personal message of best wishes or a thank you lets someone know you genuinely care about them and took time out of your full life to think about them. Use the art of writing to express yourself and connect with others with elegance, sophistication, and heart.

USING EMOTIONAL INTELLIGENCE FOR EFFECTIVE COMMUNICATION

Emotional intelligence, widely referred to as EQ, or emotional quotient, is the capacity to be aware of, control, and express one's emotions, and to handle interpersonal relationships judiciously and empathetically. Everyone can improve their emotional intelligence, and the ability to understand and read emotions is essential to mastering hospitality.

The bestselling author and psychologist Daniel Goleman explained different components of EQ, including (1) self-awareness: how to recognize and understand emotions and the sense of how one's actions, moods, and the emotions of others take effect, (2) self-regulation: understanding how to be flexible, coping with change, and how to manage conflict, (3) social skills: how to interact well with others and how it involves applying an understanding of emotions to more effectively communicate and interact with others on a daily basis, and (4) empathy: the ability to respond appropriately to other people based on recognizing their emotions.[8]

Blair Kidwell and Jonathan Hasford, in their study "Emotional Ability and Nonverbal Communication in Psychology and Marketing,"[9] discuss four dimensions of emotional ability and explain that nonverbal signals send powerful messages to others, from our overall gestures, the way we behave, how we make eye contact, how closely we stand to others, to mention just a few. Understanding and building our EQ can assist as well in problem solving in areas related to emotion: recognizing nonverbal cues and emotions in faces, understanding the meanings of emotion in words, and managing feelings. The authors elaborated further and explained four different areas that can be extremely useful in our daily job as people professionals having contact with employees and guests:

- Identify emotional content in faces, voices, and ability to accurately express emotions.
- Facilitate thinking by drawing on emotions as motivational and substantive inputs.
- Understand the meaning of emotions and their implications for behavior.
- Manage emotions in oneself and others.

I want you to reflect on how you were able to build your EQ through experience and how you have made others feel in a particular situation. You have to feel the other person's emotional state, observe them, and act upon that accordingly. Every single interaction with another person is different and allows you a chance to improve your ability to communicate like a true people person and a true hotelier—a host to guests who have different needs and are in different states of being when they stay with you.

EMPATHY AS A TOOL FOR COMMUNICATIONS

Empathy is another skill we can use as hoteliers to further help with our communication. Do you remember the expression to "put yourself in someone else's shoes?" Empathizing involves the capacity to recognize the emotions of someone else and the ability to be sensitive to another's condition or viewpoint. In a study, the authors Davidson, Pizzagalli, Nitschke, and Kalin[10] explained that a person lends one's own memory, imagination, sensitivity, and awareness toward another's experience. Empathy is when you want to clearly identify with the emotions expressed by the other person. This process takes your full attention—you need to keep focused on any sign the person gives you. Sympathy is different from empathy, and it means to understand and care for someone else's suffering.

Empathy is described as a highly disciplined and demanding state of being, involving an active and artful use of all of one's faculties of memory, imagination, sensitivity, and awareness in coming to understand another person's experience from his or her own perspective. Empathy makes it possible to resonate with other people's positive and negative feelings alike. It allows us to feel the emotions of someone else closely and intensely and gives us the ability to share those feelings. Although empathy allows you to feel connected with someone, you do not confuse yourself with the other; that is, you still know that the emotion that you resonate with is the emotion of someone else.

From my standpoint, empathy is an important ability required by any top professional. You want to fully embrace this skill to understand others. When speaking with others, think beyond yourself and your own concerns, as it is critical to make the other person the focal point. Empathizing is a critical, ongoing journey of growth and discovery. In addition, you get to appreciate others and learn through their knowledge and viewpoints. Welcome others' viewpoints and remain curious in all aspects to achieve your full potential as a professional and to further improve your abilities as a top professional in the people business.

THE ART OF CONVERSATION

As hoteliers and professionals in the people business, we have fantastic opportunities to practice the art of conversation every day. Every conversation you hold makes you a better conversationalist.

Conversation is an exchange of thoughts and ideas and requires the parties concerned to listen carefully to the words spoken, to pay attention to the body language and the potentially hidden messages that are not actually expressed out loud. Observe facial expressions and look for any clue or signs, especially emotional cues. A professional focuses their attention on the other person or persons. With this approach, you can always learn through listening and observation. Listening and observing allow us to learn, comprehend, and further develop a certain capacity to empathize. You will be surprised how much you can learn by holding a simple conversation. Clearly focus on the other person, and on yourself as well—how developed your listening skills are—then prepare appropriate answers to engage in a solid conversation.

Listening is the most important factor to success in conversation, and it clearly shows your empathy to others. You might have heard of the 80/20 rule, when you spend 80 percent of the time listening and observing and 20 percent of the time speaking. Try to focus on your own skills and ability to further fine-tune and improve your listening skills. This might not be easy at first, as we often get distracted, and most of the time we have our opinion shaped before we hear the first word spoken. Many people are often thinking of the next thing they want to say rather than focusing on what the person they are conversing with is saying. I would like you to practice this skill every day as often as you can. Repeat a few key phrases of the words you've heard to ensure that the person you communicate with understands that you've captured the meaning of what was expressed to you. This is such a useful way to show that you've been listening closely.

In order to show great empathy and to improve your emotional intelligence, you have to open yourself up a little bit more to others. A great way to demonstrate a bit more openness is when you listen to someone's experience and connect to it with a similar experience of your own. You want to engage in a dialogue and express your interest through your own experiences. When engaging in a conversation with a guest or someone you have not met before, it always gives you a great opportunity to learn something new. Even if you do not agree with what they say, remain curious to communicate effectively, ask questions and make comments. This will help you improve your overall communication skills, knowledge, empathy, and your EI.

Whenever you communicate, you want to ensure that your message was understood properly. Ask a few follow-up questions, if necessary. You may need to reemphasize certain points or areas to achieve alignment, clarity, and understanding. Last, when you finish a conversation, reach out to the other person with some closing words to thank and show appreciation for the time they took to speak with you. Again, you are the people person, the top professional, and you want to ensure that every encounter ends on a positive note, perhaps with a handshake, or depending on where you are and who the person is, by acting according to the expectation of that particular culture.

You must leave your own agenda at the door in order to truly listen—or at least put it on pause temporarily. You have to learn how to listen properly; it is absolutely fine not to answer too fast to any comment or question, as you want to really digest the content communicated to you. Practice the suggestions I've given to you above, and I guarantee you that you will improve your abilities fast. Have fun in the process as well.

Every employee can make a difference in making guests feel welcome when they communicate effectively. They will feel warmly greeted, engaged in good conversations, understood, and eager to come back for another stay.

Communication is a vital part in leadership and as you have gone through this section in great detail, the next step is to build on those competencies and strengthen your overall leadership capabilities. Principle #7 will give you the needed guidelines and information to master various leadership traits, to fine-tune your ability to lead by example, and refine your overall leadership approach.

CHAPTER THIRTEEN

PRINCIPLE #7:
DEVELOP YOUR LEADERSHIP STYLE AND STRENGTHS

The first and most important choice a leader makes is the choice to serve, without which one's capacity to lead is severely limited.
—Robert Greenleaf

As a leader, you have a role to guide, support, and inspire your team members. You can make a good or a bad impression on every employee. You can either negatively affect them or inspire them for the rest of their day. Sometimes it's just giving them an encouraging smile. Sometimes it's saying, "Thank you," and noticing something they've done well.

But there's much more to leadership than compliments and smiles. I've studied the main schools of thought regarding leadership practices and want to outline which ones I think are most adaptable to the hotel business. Each of us has to be aware of our personality, strengths, and gifts and then bring our knowledge, skills, and expertise to our place of work. Over time, we need to see what makes us most effective when interacting with others.

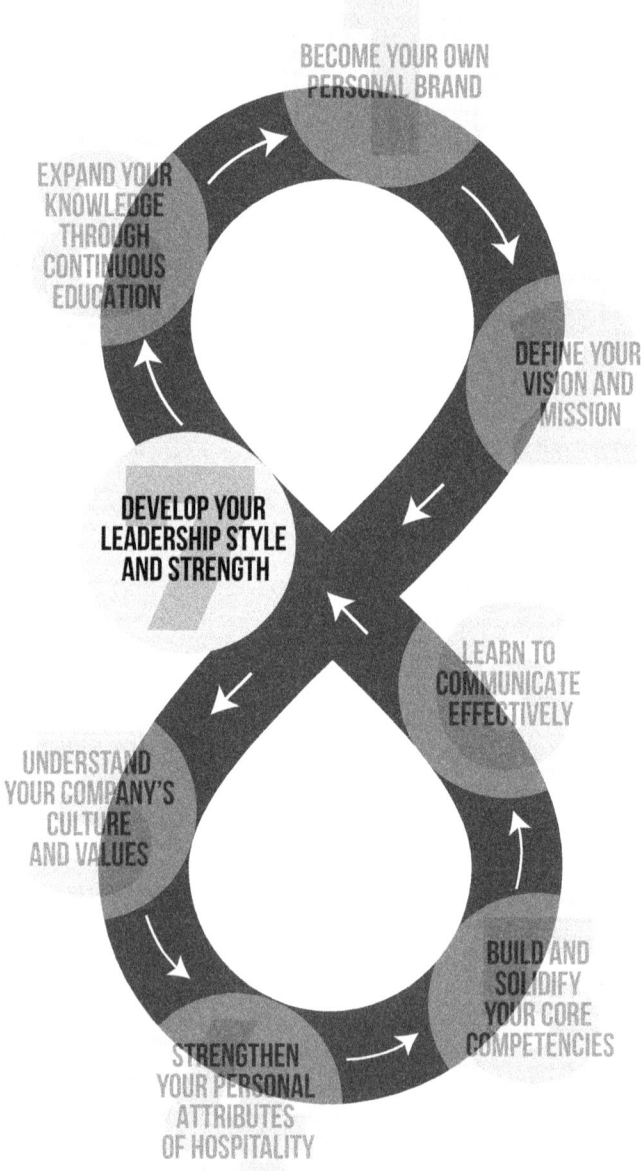

Study the various leadership principles I outline in this chapter, and see how they fit best into your daily approach to create excellence and how you can best utilize the various theories in different circumstances. Of course, no one leadership style guarantees you an ideal and desired outcome by itself. There is no one style that allows you to lead in every single situation. You have to build your abilities as an effective leader, test out the different styles, and try to apply them during your daily interactions with your team members.

The goal, of course, is to have your direct reports excel at all times—that is the art of leadership—and you will be able to make that difference with your employees by adhering to the key leadership principles and by focusing on improving the key leadership styles to achieve yours and the company's goals.

THE DIFFERENCE BETWEEN MANAGEMENT AND LEADERSHIP

I want it to be clear that both management and leadership are critical to your success—one builds on the other—but they are distinct in many aspects. Professionals need to be aware of the differences between the two but excel at both. You have to utilize your strengths as a manager to focus on your leadership skills and approach and further strengthen your leadership because you are a strong manager. At the core of an inspiring and true leader is a clear understanding of how to manage, starting with yourself. As a successful professional, you wear both hats and know how to juggle them both for the best possible outcome. It is critical that you strengthen both skill sets, which are different—yet crucial—to your overall success. Below I outline a few of the differences and discuss why you should be clearly mastering them as a future business leader.

- A leader inspires people to reach new heights by creating the vision and involving their colleagues. A manager looks at measuring the potential outcomes through establishing goals, processes, and procedures.

- A leader is focused on constant innovation, disrupting the status quo. A manager tries to keep existing processes in place by refining potential procedures to improve them.

- A leader is a risk taker and looks for new ways to improve the product and services, "breaking" the norm. A leader considers calculated failures, as this is important to create new ways of growing the business. A manager tries to limit unwanted risks, focuses on the bottom line, and tries to control problems to protect the profitability.

- A leader seeks to continuously grow professionally and personally. A manager relies more on his existing knowledge, proven skill sets, and focuses on aspects and know-how that made him or her successful. Becoming the best in your current job is critical for you to move up, but you always need to embrace a leader's ability to remain on top of your game and ahead of the competition.

- A leader creates loyal followers and has the ability to inspire others to go above and beyond to strengthen

PRINCIPLE #7: DEVELOP YOUR LEADERSHIP STYLE AND STRENGTHS

the brand and to achieve and exceed expectations. Employees look up to inspiring and successful leaders, and some may even become their role model. A manager has employees who follow guidance and directions to ensure they do not create any concerns for their boss.

There are many more examples of the differences between a leader and a manager. I want you to be able to make that distinction as you grow in your job and to embrace both as suitable and necessary for your work.

As a successful leader, you know how to learn from past experiences and take those lessons into account when focusing on the future. A great leader is a great learner and listener. You want to constantly focus on improvements, starting with yourself and inspiring others in your team and your environment to improve as well. Furthermore, you always want to focus on the solution, remaining optimistic and portraying a positive attitude to everyone. Employees want to work with inspiring, positive, trustworthy leaders who embrace challenges and listen to their team members and incorporate them into the process of change.

Your role as a true leader is to be a solid manager as well. In short, management skills overlap with leadership skills, as both involve problem solving, decision making, planning, delegation, communication, and time management. Solid managers don't always make good leaders. The critical role of a manager is to ensure that the various moving parts of a department or company are properly working together, that processes and procedures are aligned, followed, and create a smooth running of the operation.

To be a solid manager, you need to understand the business aspect of your department or hotel. Learn about and strengthen your overall skills in business organization, finance, and all the other important divisions to become successful in your current and future roles.

Based on my research, experiences, and learning from the best, I believe that two styles are critical to your success as a leader in the people business. I outline different explanations about leadership, describing leadership theories so that you can better understand their importance and differences. I then highlight and further elaborate on "servant" and "authentic" leadership styles, as these two leadership theories are at the source of your leadership success and need to be owned and understood in combination. I have also set these styles in a hotel environment, so you can get some more specific leadership lessons based in our industry.

SERVANT LEADERSHIP

In 1977 Robert Greenleaf[11] introduced the notion of servant leadership to modern organizations. The power of servant leadership lies in the leader's ability to unleash the potential and thus the power in those around. According to Dominic Cooper, servant leaders focus on others first and set employees up for success by understanding and facilitating their needs.[12] Using the servant leadership approach assists in creating an environment of trust and increases overall employee engagement, positively affecting others and the overall performance of the business unit.

In all my years in the business, the servant leadership style has become the most important when focusing on creating sustainable approaches and outcomes in any area. Perfecting this style takes a lot of personal input and requires you to become more humble. It's not about you; it's about your peers, the people you work with and for, and for everyone on whom you can have an impact.

Everyone who has ever worked in housekeeping understands its importance and challenges for any hotel. Hotels are judged by their cleanliness, particularly in guests' rooms, and if a guest's room is not clean, it's unlikely that guest will want to come back to your hotel. To guarantee a safe and clean environment at all times, leadership—and servant leadership in particular—plays an important role. The employees in housekeeping perform extremely hard work on a daily basis; it's repetitive, hard, physical labor. Most of the employees often have just a basic level of education (this is not always true, but often), and requires leadership that can engage and empathize properly.

A leader needs to create a work environment where constant support—both emotional and physical—is given and constantly connect with the staff to create a supportive and happy team. A servant leader steps in when necessary and has the professional capability to engage, listen, understand, and empathize with the issues their employees are grappling with. A servant leader should be great at communicating and have the ability to build upon everyone's strengths and inspire their team by doing the work themself if necessary. Leaders must be able to sense if a housekeeper needs assistance, further training, and if and where it is critical to step in and make the staff member or anyone on the team more successful.

This is true not only in housekeeping: all employees need to feel supported, understood, and inspired to add value to the guest's stay, not only through a clean room, but by showing and demonstrating clear commitment to create memories through value-added services. For any employee to go above and beyond, leaders need to recognize, praise, and back their team members.

A great leader understands how to read the obvious and sometimes hidden signs of an employee's well-being, to carefully listen and empathize. A servant leader puts the interest of the employees first and understands how to make them feel proud of their work. At the end of the day, an employee needs to feel appreciated and inspired to come back the next day and execute the work in an even better way.

My first job with my current employer was as the manager of housekeeping, and I spent a lot of time with each team member, helping with the rooms, simply pitching in—stripping the beds, wiping down tables, emptying the trash, replacing the towels. This gave me a great opportunity to engage with these associates, to get to know them better, to show support, and to make them understand how important they were to the hotel and to me. I told them how I admired their work ethic and explained how their work is absolutely critical in creating a phenomenal hotel. I tried to learn from them as well about how management could assist them better.

As a leader, I stopped by different employees during the day, not looking for mistakes, but focusing on all the hard work they did; this was a great opportunity to show my appreciation and dedication to them. I never just walked by any of the rooms, but always stopped, greeted the employees, looked for ways to help (without making them uncomfortable), to get to know them better and recognize them for all their efforts.

Due to my daily engagement with them, I built trust, showed them authenticity, appreciation, and tried to demonstrate that their growth and happiness was my most important way to say thank you. It allowed me to strengthen the team, because my interest was the well-being of the employees. Spending equal time with people is critical, but sometimes it requires further assistance, training, and support to teach and grow particular individuals. My leadership style was an example to others and the team became a solid, cohesive, inspired workforce, excited to learn and grow.

"I am here for you" is an important phrase in a servant leader's life and one of my personal mantras. A servant leader is someone who brings a ray of sunshine to other people's hearts.

AUTHENTIC LEADERSHIP

Authentic leadership is influenced by the ethical behavior of a leader and comprises self-awareness of a leader; she knows her strengths and weaknesses and makes positive relationships with employees by inspiring and encouraging them. According to Bruce Avolio and William Gardner, authentic leaders are insightful and self-aware and have high ethical and moral standards.[13] Those leaders are highly aware of their beliefs and how these values influence others, engaging in a balanced decision-making approach and presenting their genuine selves to others. Authentic leadership, explains Hannes Leroy, et al, occurs when individuals enact their true selves in their role as a leader and when leaders are being honest with themselves and sincere with others.[14] Authentic leaders invest in solid relationships, have strong connections with others, and share their experiences with others to create mutual trust.

I learned early on that there is no shortcut to creating sustainable excellence and that it takes focus, determination, empathy, and professionalism to drive results accordingly. During my many years in the food and beverage department (F&B), I learned to listen and observe carefully, especially from the great culinary professionals I've had the honor of working with, that true excellence is created by authenticity, both on the plate and through engagement with employees and guests.

A true chef always wants to present their best self in their culinary presentations, preparing food with care, precision, and knowledge that they are always up to the task to make a delicious meal. A chef knows what is in season, how to best stir the senses of a guest with their creations, whether they be a taste of the local area or a taste of home that the guest or patron might be missing.

Authentic chefs inspire their followers, including me, because they stay true to their values and believe in their craft. They know who they are and understand the value of teaching and inspiring others, bringing their passion to life.

Great maitre d's aim to create a trusted environment for employees and guests alike. They demonstrate their authenticity when teaching and mentoring staff and when they present themselves to patrons and stakeholders, explaining ingredients and the tastes of their favorite dish or describing a particular wine with enthusiasm and competence. Every time we are with guests, we have an opportunity to create an MM (memory moment), through our passion, genuine desire to make guests happy, and our ability to lead by example. An authentic leader inspires loyalty and trust in others and creates unmatched bonds that last a lifetime.

I've always admired top professionals in F&B/Culinary because of their ability to be themselves; they understand that consistency comes only through authenticity, commitment, personal engagement, professionalism, and vision to focus on bigger and better things. I improved my authentic leadership style through being true to who I am—always aiming to become a better professional. An employee wants to work, learn, and grow through leaders who have the know-how, the empathy, who say what they believe in (with diplomacy, of course) but always keep true to oneself and in line with the company value system. I strongly believe that an authentic leader builds trust through credibility and always has the best in mind for the employees.

I learned to be around the employees during the busy times in F&B, engaging and assisting, and tried to make them better professionally, to ensure that they can learn and grow and to further their confidence. I saw many employees improve and gave them the opportunity to take care of the guests accordingly, creating not only inspired employees and happy customers, but strengthening the team spirit and overall business outcome. Guests want to be surrounded by professionals, so the overall experience needs to be flawless and in alignment with the brand promise.

I strongly believe that authenticity shows the real heart of a leader, requiring a clear understanding and identification with their values. An authentic leader is genuine and true to their beliefs. An authentic leader is purpose-driven and never compromises on their value system. These leaders know who they are and why they are doing what they do. An authentic leader leads with both their heart and mind, as both complement each other. I learned that authenticity in a leader is critical, as they do not just follow instructions but use their expertise, compassion, and conviction to create long-term connections with team members. An authentic leader is self-driven, demonstrates great discipline, walks the talk, and is never too shy to defend what is most important.

TRANSACTIONAL LEADERSHIP

The transactional leadership style mostly focuses on the transactions between a leader and the team members. I have often experienced this type of leadership where the entire tone and the actions are more authoritative. Transactional leadership is useful in environments where employees need to follow stricter processes and rules. There are many examples within a hotel environment where this style is necessary to align everyone on key procedures and expectations. A transactional leader guides followers to achieve competency in specific tasks and applies a reward system to keep everyone inspired to achieve continuity and excellence.

Although it is important to understand why this leadership style has its place, I strongly believe that it should never be used as a sole style and is better applied to make a point in certain situations. Again, the key leadership styles are "servant" and "authentic," and knowing how and when to use and apply other styles like "transactional" and "transformational" leadership to achieve desired results is key.

Let's look at an example of how transactional leadership works at the front desk, where guests are greeted by the staff and are checked in. Hotel workers want to be as efficient as possible doing this task, while creating a welcoming atmosphere for the guest. As in all other areas of the hotel, competency and efficiency are key focal points for a transactional leadership approach.

When I worked at the front desk, effectiveness was key, as guests wanted to get their room keys as fast as possible and begin to relax, get to their meeting, or start sightseeing. The first few weeks on the job, I needed to learn all the basic elements of a perfect check-in, including the computer program and how to interact with customers and meet their expectations. Later, as a manager in this area, I needed to continuously work with the employees to fine-tune the technical elements of their job. I had to ensure that everyone, with every guest, flawlessly went through all the procedures to execute a successful check-in. Oftentimes, I stood next to the employees and checked every single step, listened to the conversation with the guests, and ensured that there were no concerns with the step-by-step approach of the transaction. This was critical to give clear feedback to my team to ensure that the overall process went more smoothly with practice.

In my role as a manager, I learned to be very specific in my communication and how to listen more carefully and was therefore able to guide, correct, and assist the employees to become more effective. It was clear that the staff needed to fully comprehend the processes and make it more routine to achieve better speed, more competency, allowing them to engage customers more personally and with ease in the process.

It takes a true leader to inspire employees to be excited about what is a very repetitive work process. Learning by doing becomes absolutely critical. I explained to the employees that it is a little bit like starting out how to tap-dance (which I did when I was sixteen). First, it's vital to master the steps properly and in a way that you can perform them almost in your sleep. It takes practice, practice, practice, and that was the expectation for everyone.

Once the "technical" side was clear and almost automated, with their fingers flying over the computer keys and moving the mouse, the real performance and show started. Then, like in tap dancing, you could free the feet from the upper body and let go to impress through style, elegance, and artistic ability, which meant that you put on a confident smile when you know the routine perfectly; you can look at the audience, show confidence, and make them feel that they are in capable hands.

In any job function and position, you will experience similar factors, and transactional leadership is crucial to have a smooth running of the operation, again, with skills, confidence, and performance. With any leadership style, the leader needs to know and feel when to recognize the employees. Transactional work processes might seem more "dry" in nature; therefore it is even more important that leaders understand how and when to recognize an employee for a job well done.

TRANSFORMATIONAL LEADERSHIP

The transformational approach is a step up from transactional leadership, incorporating more specific involvement from the leader to keep the motivation of the employees at the highest possible level and inspiring them to go further. I learned this trade from top professionals, and I always felt that they knew how to push me harder and higher, but in an inspirational way. I always wanted more to make my leader proud.

As a leader with sales responsibilities, I learned how to inspire my team members to work harder and smarter. I learned also how to lead change by being an example and by teaching, energizing, and guiding employees to achieve their own goals, while at the same time contributing to the division's success. Developing others was critical, and I was highly rewarded by competent and happy employees who were reaching new heights and supporting others to achieve excellence.

I was thrilled to see the development of my team members as they built on past successes to move up and become successful in their own right. Through my ability to combine the various approaches and to excel as a leader, I gained their trust and respect. I knew that I had to win their hearts and minds to make them better professionals so they could achieve their own ambitions. My goal for them was to have their own clear vision and approach to success, the ability to manage their tasks well, to achieve greater heights through professionalism, commitment, enthusiasm, joy for the job, and their contributions to the hotel.

For any successful leader, building solid relationships with employees, peers, and other stakeholders is absolutely key to a successful long-term relationship. I strongly believe that transformational leadership is a vital and basic part of leadership. During my career, the most essential route I've seen to achieving sustainable success with others is building a trusting relationship where you as the leader demonstrate competency at all times and walk the talk. In many ways, you can only be called a leader if you show to others that you care, focus on their growth, and commit to goals by leading the efforts personally, with enthusiasm, professionalism, and inspiration.

SERVANT AND AUTHENTIC LEADERSHIP STYLES AS KEY TO YOUR LEADERSHIP SUCCESS

As mentioned before, the two key leadership styles that will make you the best possible leader are the servant leader and authentic leader. I cannot reiterate enough how critical it is

PRINCIPLE #7: DEVELOP YOUR LEADERSHIP STYLE AND STRENGTHS

for you to embrace those theories, identify with their styles, and ensure that you fully understand and implement them to achieve sustainable success. You have the opportunity to constantly practice, improve, and strengthen your styles in every single interaction. You need to measure the outcome based on desired results, through creating a work environment where the employees feel that they can create excellence for themselves, their peers, and all stakeholders. With these two leadership styles in combination, and with learning from others, you will absolutely excel in your endeavor to become the best leader that you can be.

It is now up to you to further refine your leadership competencies based on this principle. I have no doubt that you will achieve your goal to become not only a solid mentor and leader, but that many will choose you to become their role model.

Once you have achieved a certain mastery in a particular job or position, and by embracing the various principles to assist you with your continued growth, you will want to reflect on the next career step. As I have done throughout my journey, I always analyzed my competency-gap and tried to fill it either through internal training opportunities, self-learning, additional exposure to other areas of the business, or through further education. The last principle, #8, will guide you on the importance of additional courses and programs for you to be ready and excited about more responsibilities, giving you an edge and the needed proficiency to get a step closer to your dream job!

CHAPTER FOURTEEN
PRINCIPLE #8:
EXPAND YOUR KNOWLEDGE THROUGH CONTINUOUS EDUCATION

We must become the change we want to see.
—Mahatma Gandhi

I am very proud of you that you already went through the prior principles to become better and stronger as a professional. Please take a moment to congratulate yourself and reflect on your journey so far to become a more competent YOU! As I've mentioned on several occasions, continued education is a critical element and principle to achieve mastery. Principle #8 is at the end of the first cycle, and as the number represents a never-ending loop, you will continue back to Principle #1 and again be backquestioning your current state, and then strengthening your overall abilities!

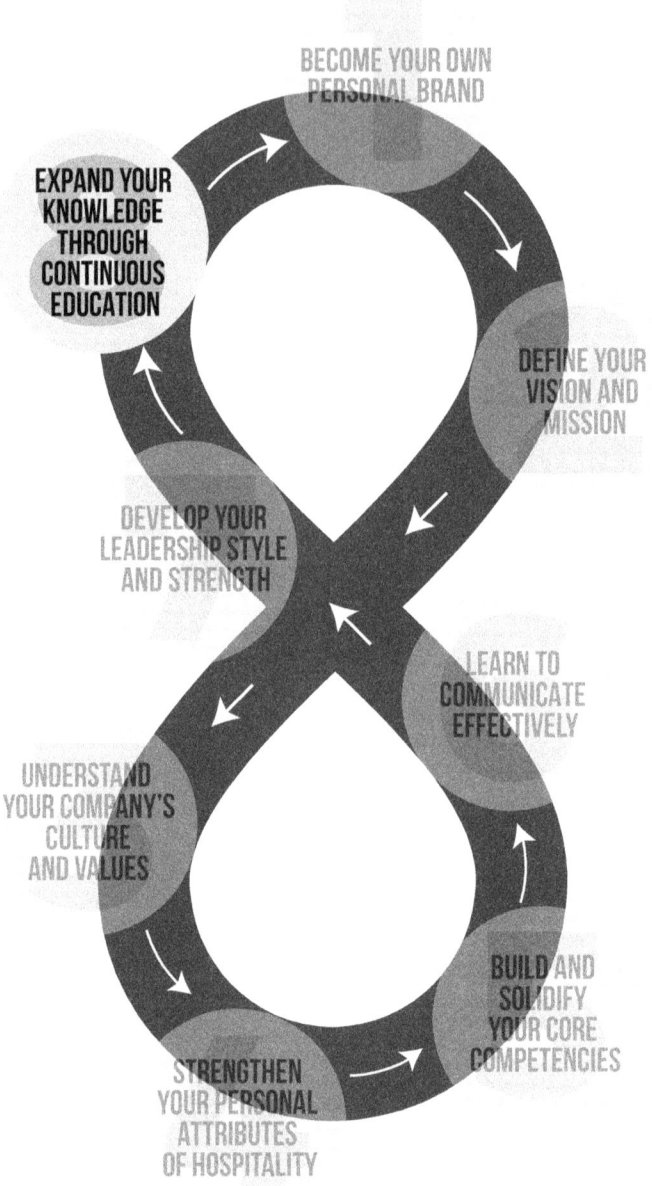

PRINCIPLE #8: EXPAND YOUR KNOWLEDGE THROUGH CONTINUOUS EDUCATION

Creating an environment of constant learning is vital to the success of any organization and any individual. It's been proven that effective training and talent development helps increase overall productivity and creates a desirable work environment, reduces turnover, and therefore improves product and service quality and the profitability of the department or company. As I have seen throughout my career, employees, peers, and team members are eager to learn, excited to focus on improving their future prospects, and embrace a leadership approach based on individual talents and employee-specific improvement plans.

Challenge your human resources and training leaders to assist you with the best training tools, and ask your manager to give you access to a library or courses for you to improve your professional skills. In my earlier years, I had to do my own research, as training opportunities were somewhat limited and not well organized. At that time, online learning was not widespread, and one of the only ways to really focus on growth was through business books and mentorship. I learned a lot from Stephen Covey and his book *The 7 Habits of Highly Effective People*. I would recommend it for anyone—some hotel companies offer courses from this book.

I've always enjoyed learning on the job, as I could immediately see if something I've done is working. This aspect of learning and growing is a proven approach, which I will elaborate on further in this chapter.

There are many ways you can learn and grow in any organization. It is important that you focus on a way to build your skills that makes sense for the anticipated growth of your career and go over this plan with your key leader and mentor. In general, human resources and the training department offer—or should offer—regular classes about the company culture, the brand, classroom workshops about various leadership topics or other key subjects relevant to the growth of employees and aspiring and current leaders. Those trainings are more general, but important to strengthen basic management skills, create alignment, as well as build a coherent brand culture. It is important to participate in these workshops. You might even be called in to give your input or expertise on a particular subject.

As much as the human resources department is responsible for those types of training opportunities, you also need to focus on filling the competency gap with learning specific to where you need to train. Classroom style is always important, but the most effective training is on the job. As mentioned throughout the book, you want to become an expert at what you currently do. To achieve this goal, take a proactive approach to your own growth and express your need and wishes to the people who can make a difference for you. There are various ways you can do this. I highlight the most important ones below.

On-the-job training is one of the most basic and powerful employee development methods within hospitality, or really within any industry. Everyone learns by doing, and you want to be on high alert by observing and mirroring a great employee who has the skills you are looking to acquire. It takes a solid mentor or a "buddy" at work who can guide you, show you,

PRINCIPLE #8: EXPAND YOUR KNOWLEDGE THROUGH CONTINUOUS EDUCATION

correct you, and support you. This can help you gain confidence fast and learn about the job with every single step.

Other forms of employee training include role-playing, where you group several employees together and engage in real-life scenarios, as well as internet-based training, which enables employees to train at their own pace at a time and place that is convenient to them.

Leaders have to watch out not to "lose" employees because they do not get the training opportunities and required leadership involvement as "promised" through the company culture and expected by employees.

Another way of gaining knowledge is through self-directed learning. Do not underestimate this important and powerful tool. You will always find time (based on your time management plan) to enroll in a course important to you. Again, please do not wait until someone proposes it to you. Be proactive, because you know what you require, but reach out to experts to understand how to spend your time productively and wisely.

I encourage you in your spare time to ask for an opportunity to get trained or exposed to another area of the hotel or the business. If you currently work at the Front Desk, and you want to grow in other areas of the Rooms Division, in Rooms, and you feel that growth in F&B is important to improve your overall understanding of the business, then voice your interest and spend time with other teams to learn. Not only does that show you are interested in being knowledgeable about other parts of the hotel, but leaders can see your initiative and your drive. As a leader, you never want to prevent anyone with drive, enthusiasm, and real motivation from growing. Please work on your development plan constantly, refine it, get help from your superior, voice your opinion, excitement, and interest, and don't let anyone stop you.

You will never be the role model you want to be—one who is identified by fellow employees, peers, and other professionals—without properly understanding the technical aspects of your job, so learn, learn, and learn, and then practice, practice, practice.

I remember when I worked in a hotel in the United States, we had a lot of famous sports teams staying with us. Athletes have incredible discipline and focus on continuous improvement. The NBA basketball players play eighty-two games in a season, forty-one of which are played on the road. In my talks with them, it was interesting to hear that in their mindset, success was yesterday, and today is a new opportunity and obligation to do it even better. Once you are a top player (like I want you to become in the hotel business), you have no excuse not to perform at your best. I've witnessed basketball, ice hockey, and football greats reassemble as a team to go over the game, look at concerns, highlights, successes, and to further focus on improvements. Some even head to the gym to practice afterward, to focus on their personal approach to excellence, strengthening their skills or muscles, to become even better and stronger.

Top athletes, famous actors, musicians, and entertainers, understand where they are lacking, where they have opportunities, and on what, where, and when they have to work harder and smarter to outshine others. They have an incredible discipline and focus on constant improvement. No wonder these people remain on top of their game for such a long period of time and become the heroes we all look up to. I've been really fortunate to meet a lot of them during my career.

MOVING ON TO HIGHER EDUCATION

After years of learning all I could and always striving to reach higher, I gradually moved up the ranks in the company and achieved a major milestone to become a general manager in one of the company's luxury hotels in China. This was an incredible step forward, and my dream came true. I'll never forget my meeting with the vice president when he offered me the GM job. This was a highlight in my professional and personal life and a milestone I was working toward for a long time.

The incredible thing was that even though I'd been preparing to become a general manager, once I actually started taking over a hotel, I felt like I should have learned so much more during my earlier years to help me out in my new position. Once you are on top, you need to perform. People expect you to be somewhat fully prepared for your new responsibilities. I quickly saw that I had deficiencies, but I was lucky enough to have coworkers who complemented my senior leadership team perfectly and balanced out my shortcomings. This allowed me to further grow in the position and execute strategies based on my strengths and the strengths of the team members.

This is what you really need to learn: Standing alone you will never succeed. You need the right people around you who complement your weaker sides. As you build your career, you will become great at what your natural talents are, and to a certain degree, you will remain weaker at other professional competencies that are not naturally your interests and strong points. This is fine, as long you clearly understand your strengths and shortcomings and you can lead others with authenticity, enthusiasm, and inspiration to succeed as a team.

After a successful two years as a general manager and a great hotel opening, and becoming the market leader in all business matrixes within a short period of time, I realized that I wanted to further strengthen my business acumen and continue my education to achieve even greater heights. I was searching for executive MBA courses online and was happy to discover a new way of learning by starting classes at a university in California. Almost ten years ago, the hotel business was not really focused on letting their senior employees continue their studies. It was mostly unnecessary, many of the leaders told me, but the ones who realized the potential in my gaining further education absolutely supported me in my quest to graduate with an executive MBA (EMBA).

It was a tough task to manage the hotel business and responsibilities with family and schoolwork. It took me about fifteen to twenty hours a week to prepare and work on school matters, and it was clear that I could not compromise on work and family. I learned also that I needed balance and still needed to do my workouts.

PRINCIPLE #8: EXPAND YOUR KNOWLEDGE THROUGH CONTINUOUS EDUCATION

I'm passionate about going to the gym and kickboxing. This was the best way for me to maintain a happy and healthy life.

I believe that many people make the mistake of enrolling too early in their careers to earn an MBA. Enticing young managers to earn an MBA has become a big business for universities but I strongly believe it is not as valuable as many people think, particularly in the earlier years of your career. You can find MBA courses everywhere and without needed qualifications in the business. One or two years of working in a supervisor or manager position are simply not enough. It takes you more time and years to complete your journey on the job before you should go back and fine-tune your business competencies. You have to ask yourself what you expect from a higher degree. What is it that you want to get from it?

Earning an executive MBA (EMBA) was more valuable at the right time, as it required me to have solid work and leadership experience to qualify, compared to a regular MBA. The decision was clear as most EMBA students are executives in their own fields, which can add a lot of value to the studies because of the different levels of experience that are brought to the table. A commitment of two years of study is huge, and like with everything else, you want to get the most out of it. You do not want to simply spend money to have an academic accomplishment without the needed competencies to bring you further. I am not saying that a regular MBA is a bad thing. But it makes more sense to pursue an EMBA once you are skilled and experienced in your profession. Once you are in the right place in your career, join a solid school with the appropriate curriculum to teach you what you cannot learn easily in the work environment. Particularly when it comes to serious overall business knowledge, it would be best to find a program with colleagues who have other areas of expertise, making the classes more exciting and challenging.

LEARNING ABOUT INNOVATIONS IN BUSINESS SCHOOL

The hotel industry needs to continuously evolve and still has great opportunities to further grow through innovation. I am always amazed when I read about the hotel business in César Ritz's times (see chapter two on the history of hotels). They invented the restaurant business almost as it is now, by presenting menus to guests who can choose their liking. One hundred and fifty years later, we somehow still do the same, although there is now a new trend, particularly in smaller restaurants, where you can order online and on your mobile phone.

There are many ways in our business to be proactive and innovate as part of the broader mindset. Several incremental innovations have occurred over the years and made a big impact on consumers. But compared to other industries, the hotel business has further chances to improve. One important aspect that will never go away, though, and will become even more important with a more digitalized world, is the personal touch, the competence of the employees, inspiring leadership, and the ability and willingness to create exceptional memories.

Future opportunities are being created right now thanks to new and improved technologies, including artificial intelligence. I can see this development here in China clearly. Changes happen constantly; for example, guests have started to pay their bills through apps on their mobile phones, and they can now even order room service from outside vendors through particular online food and beverage providers. It is clear that this trend is difficult to stop.

Many of these new technologies present fantastic opportunities for businesses, and many companies have already embraced those innovations for their own advantage. Virtual reality, for example, offers great possibilities for numerous areas in the hotel. Lodging companies work together with industry experts to fine-tune this type of technology to offer virtual trips through various areas of the hotel and create an advantage over the competition. There is a great chance now to leapfrog and create offerings and services that incorporate the new tools available. Hotels need to learn how to utilize these modern advancements together with our own skill sets to provide products that are better suited for the needs of an ever-changing customer base.

So what is the takeaway here? Let's learn from the best, as well as look outside the fence of our industry, not only to experience and capture what they did but how they got there in the first place and what drives them to continuously challenge the status quo to innovate, to exceed expectations, and to amaze customers through product and service innovation.

You clearly manage your own future and future development, and I am not saying that you need an EMBA or any other master's or higher education. There are a multitude of other solid courses and degrees that could be beneficial to you.

Many hotel schools and other business schools offer certificate courses, which I believe can add great value to know-how, professional, and personal growth. I have improved through Cornell's programs, and I believe they have a lot of great benefits. Cornell is not the only school to offer these programs. Please check the various options and see how one of these two-to-three month courses (or even longer) can fit into your schedule, based on your desired growth and objectives. It is not up to me to tell you what you need, as that is based on your current skill sets and desired future goals, as you'll have written in your personal vision and mission statement, but continued improvements and learning is key to a solid future as a leader.

I want you to choose the ideal school with the right courses for you to achieve your ultimate goal. Be critical when you make a selection for any school, and ask the right questions to the admissions' office, or anyone who is able and willing to give you advice and feedback about any of the programs. A good way to do this is to go through alumni. I selected my EMBA due to its curriculum, the broad student base, its international reach, and because I wanted to be surrounded by non-hoteliers, as it was not a hotel-sponsored school; nor were the courses hotel related. This was because I wanted to be with professionals from other industries, so I could learn about their approach to overall

PRINCIPLE #8: EXPAND YOUR KNOWLEDGE THROUGH CONTINUOUS EDUCATION

business, their understanding of the various subject matters, and because I wanted to break out from the norm of the hotel industry. I was with like-minded executives who added value to my learning (and I hope vice versa), as they had the same intention as I. You want to be challenged, and you need to be questioned by faculty and peers to further improve and achieve the best possible result.

I strongly believe that all of us in the business need and should immerse ourselves into other industries and learn from top experts and leaders. And I tried to do just that. I had the opportunity to be in a class with experienced business owners, mostly from the tech companies in Silicon Valley, who had been busy creating companies. Two of my classmates were already in their late fifties and wanted to finally have a degree. They'd made enough money in the earlier tech years and had now become "angel investors" for young and aspiring companies. I felt lucky and happy during those two years, as the experience opened my eyes and ears even wider and allowed me to learn and grow from experts in various fields. All the courses were interactive, and it was crucial to add value to everyone in the class through well-thought-out and solid comments and contributions.

I achieved my goal and look at any business issue differently than I did before. I learned that making things better is not just expected, but making things absolutely the best is the key to long-term success.

When facing and analyzing a business problem, it should always be an opportunity to further improve the product, processes, and eventually, the staffs' competencies working on these issues. In our industry, we seem to look at an employee, guest, or process breakdown as painful tasks, and there are those who will try to take shortcuts instead of embracing the opportunity to make sustainable improvements of the product, eventually strengthening stakeholders' professionalism and overall brand positioning of the hotel and company. This is the reason why I included the total quality management approach in earlier chapters. This practice was not invented by hoteliers for hoteliers, but it is critical for all of us and all in any business to sustainably improve processes, products, and overall services.

GETTING A DOCTORATE

I was happy and satisfied with my EMBA, but I always knew that I had more opportunities to improve my overall knowledge, leadership skills, and to add more value to the people I work with. I was interested in furthering my studies, to achieve a doctorate in business administration (DBA). After a one-year break from school, I enrolled in my next school, the DBA program at Walden University. Why a doctorate? Well, simply because I was motivated to go above and beyond and to explore territory that few in our industry have explored.

Several individuals who call themselves hoteliers have not started in the business initially, but got their degrees and even PhDs and were able to move up the ladder in big organizations as a result.

PRINCIPLE #8: EXPAND YOUR KNOWLEDGE THROUGH CONTINUOUS EDUCATION

There is absolutely nothing wrong with this approach, as the industry needs strong individuals who look at the business through a different lens. Innovation is key to move forward, and those individuals definitely brought new ideas and were able to benchmark many processes from different industries. I strongly believe that many of them made the hotel business better, but not all of them. In the end, I am persuaded that hospitality is absolutely unique, and it requires the right talent to succeed in the long run: people who live the hotel business!

I wanted to start a new chapter and immerse myself in the world of leadership, business, and hotel literature from a doctoral perspective. Over almost five years, I studied hundreds of documents, research, websites, companies in all different industries, and I wanted to get the best viewpoint of the actual state of the business. I wanted to capture the essence of the "state of the hotel business" and seek exciting and new opportunities from other industries. I learned new viewpoints, got to know many incredible people from all sorts of domains, and learned how the top companies understand their business inside and out but incorporate critical aspects, processes, and most importantly, leadership aspects that make a difference for all stakeholders throughout the organization. I got really excited about all the learning and was able to finish my studies with a comprehensive doctoral thesis pertaining to our industry, particularly focused, but not solely, on China.

Continuous education needs to be part of any leader's curriculum, and I really hope that you consider, at the right time in your career, and based on your plan, going back to school for an additional degree. It might be too early for some, and for the others, believe me, it's never too late to further grow your knowledge. As a leader, you have the absolute responsibility and duty to contribute *constantly* to the growth and success of the employees and organization, and in an ever-changing environment, with global tensions and opportunities, you can make that difference. I strongly believe that you and your family will be very proud of all your achievements. I am—and I will be for you!

FINAL WORDS

My thoughts and knowledge about the business and the journey to your own leadership excellence is important to me. I want you to be absolutely clear and excited about the prospects, the multitude of opportunities you have, and for you to work on the best possible approach to achieve all your goals, eventually to become the best leader, manager, or businessperson that you can be. The aforementioned topics are clear foundations for you to add the needed knowledge and value to be focused on what is important and to ensure that you never lose sight of your desired goals and dreams.

The key to your own growth is to take the learning and opportunities mentioned in this book and use them as a guideline in your professional and personal journey to excellence. I want you to practice, fine-tune competencies, and always remain curious and open to learn more.

The world is a fascinating place, and I want you to embrace it as a great opportunity to improve, contribute, create excitement, and spread your wealth of knowledge, happiness, and joy to others.

In our business, people make the difference. You will become the best in the people business, and I am so very excited to be part—even a little bit—of your growth and success. I learned early on in my career that contributing to others gives me great joy and pleasure, makes me a better person and a more complete leader. It is a wonderful feeling when you can assist other team members, people that need your help or assistance, and to simply touch other people's hearts when working together or trying to make a positive impact.

People will never forget when you voluntarily step forward, support, contribute, and assist others. It can be simple things, like giving a lending hand to one of your server colleagues, a leader who needs support with paperwork, a housekeeper who is in need of more supplies that you can quickly fetch for them, or anyone who would love to see you because you naturally make them feel good about themselves. I mentioned on various occasions that the power in our business lies in giving a smile to someone, and true leaders never ask if they can help someone else—they sense it, and they step in and up with great enthusiasm, motivation, and joy.

I am here to assist you, hopefully as one of your role models, as someone who has never stopped learning and who has gone through various steps and processes in my own journey to become the best that I can be. Looking back at my career, I would have loved to have had someone I could reach out to assist me with my journey to excellence, apart from the leaders in various hotels, someone who was neutral, not part of our organization, and a professional who has most probably gone through the same issues. It is my honor to help guide you to achieve your own goals and professional dreams.

I want every person, no matter what endeavor they are pursuing, to reach their fullest potential at the highest possible level. Please visit my website at www.drhotelier.com and contact me with questions, thoughts, and stories of your own successes. I will be more than happy to assist and guide you, and celebrate all your wonderful achievements with you.

—Your Dr. Hotelier, Iwan Dietschi

ENDNOTES

1 www.kendall.edu/blog/history-of-the-hospitality-industry/

2 Levy-Bonvin, Jacques. Hotels: A Brief History. December 15, 2003. www.hospitalitynet.org/opinion/4017990.html

3 https://intelity.com/blog/a-brief-look-at-the-history-of-hotel-technology/

4 Golder, P. N, Mitra, D., and Moorman, C. "What Is Quality? An Integrative Framework of Processes and States." *Journal of Marketing* Vol 76 (July 2012), 1-23.

5 Jing, G. "Diagnosing Corporate Culture Construction Problems in China." *International Journal of Business and Management* 10, no. 6 (2015) 234–238. doi:10.5539/ijbm.v10n6p234.

6   Pinho, J. C., A. P. Rodrigues, and S. Dibb. "The Role of Corporate Culture, Market Orientation and Organisational Commitment in Organisational Performance." *Journal of Management Development* 33, no. 4 (April 2014): 374–398. doi:10.1108/JMD-03-2013-0036.

7   Schwartz, M. S. (2013). "Developing and Sustaining an Ethical Corporate Culture: The Core Elements." *Business Horizons* 56, no. 1 (2013): 39–50. doi:10.1016/j.bushor.2012.09.002.

8   Goleman, D. *Emotional Intelligence: Why It Matters More Than IQ*. New York: Bantam, 1995.

9   Kidwell, B. and Hasford, J. "Emotional Ability and Nonverbal Communication." *Psychology and Marketing* 31(7) (July 2014).

10 Davidson, R. J., D. Pizzagalli, J. B Nitschke, and N. H. Kalin. "Parsing the Subcomponents of Emotion and Disorders of Emotion: Perspective from Affective Neuroscience." In R. J. Davidson, K. R. Scherer, H. H. Goldsmith (Eds.), Handbook of Affective Sciences (pp. 8–24). New York: Oxford University Press, 2003.

11 Greenleaf, R. K. Servant Leadership: A Journey into the Nature of Legitimate Power and Greatness. New York, NY: Paulist Press, 1977.

12 Cooper, D. "Effective Safety Leadership: Understanding Types & Styles That Improve Safety Performance." Professional Safety 60, no. 1 (February 2015): 49–53. Retrieved from http://www.asse.org/professional-safety.

13 Avolio B. J., and W. L. Gardner. "Authentic Leadership Development: Getting to the Root of Positive Forms of Leadership." *The Leadership Quarterly* 16 (2005): 315–338. doi:10.1016/j.leaqua.2005.03.001.

14 Leroy, H., F. Anseel, W. L. Gardner, and L. Sels. (2015). "Authentic Leadership, Authentic Followership, Basic Need Satisfaction, and Work Role Performance: A cross-Level Study." *Journal of Management* 41, no. 6 (2015): 1677–1697. doi:10.1177/0149206312457822.

INDEX

A
accountants, 134
Alibaba, 184
Amabile, Teresa M., 182
Apple, 45
apprenticeships, 19–20, 24
apps, 42, 56, 233
arrival areas, 55, 57–58
artificial intelligence (AI), 46, 233
Asia, 41
athletes, 228
authentic leadership, 213–217, 221
authenticity, 88, 156, 167, 213, 215
author
    apprenticeship, 19–20
    background, 15–18
    in China, 31, 43, 229
    in Dubai, 29
    early hotel work, 20–22, 25, 100–103, 212–213, 217–218
    education, 21–25, 100–101
    in F&B areas, 215–216
    first jobs, 19
    global experiences, 29–32
    as housekeeping manager, 28–29
    on leadership experiences, 220
    and music, 18–19, 132, 177–178
    parents, 16–17

autonomy, and creativity, 182
Avolio, Bruce, 214

B
Baden, Switzerland, 15, 36–37
Badrutt, Caspar, 39
balance, 116–118
banquet spaces, 61
Basel, Switzerland, 37
"beginner's mind", 31
Buffet, Warren, 153
business/entrepreneurial mindset, 83–84
business travel, 40

C
careers
   and dreams, 99–100, 108, 147
   early, 101–102
   opportunities, 108–109
   planning, 105, 142–143
   studying companies, 102–103
catering, 61–62
   See also food/beverage (F&B) areas; hotel restaurants
charisma, 162–163
check-in/out, 55, 217–218
chefs, 214–215
China, 31, 40–43, 229, 233
   Astor Hotel, 38–39
   FlyZoo Hotel, 42, 45
   Huazhu Hotels Group, 41
   Jin Jiang hotels, 41
cleanliness, 64, 211

club lounges, 58
communication, *122*, 124, 174–176, 184, 191, *192*, 193
   conversation, 200–203
   and emotional intelligence, 196–198
   empathy, 198–200
   non-verbal, 193–195
   written, 195–196
   See also presentations
companies, 105, *122*
competency gaps, 226
concierge services, 58
confidence, 163
constructive criticism, 93–94
continuing education, 110–111, 117, *122*, 222–223, *224*, 225–228, 237–238
   See also higher education
conversation, 200–203
Cooper, Dominic, 210
core competencies, *122*, 134, 144, 169, *170*, 171–172
Cornell, 234
corporate cultures, 27, 124, 149, *150*, 151–153, 156, 227
corporate values, 149, *150*, 157
corporate vision, 154
Covey, Stephen, 95, 144, 225
creative thinking, 181–185
creativity, 182–183
credibility, 152, 163
credit cards, 45
critical thinking, 185–189
cross-training, 227–228
cultural norms, 194–195
curiosity, 165–166

customer choices, 51
customer satisfaction, 80, 171
customer service, 184–185
customers, 164

D
Davidson, R. J., 198–199
departure experiences, 56, 66–67
Dibb, S., 152
diplomacy, 164
dream jobs, 147
Dubai, 29

E
École Hôtelière de Lausanne (EHL), 21, 23–25, 44, 100–101
    See also hotel schools
eight, 123
Eight Principles for Excellence, 121, *122*, 123, 125, *128*, *140*, *150*, *160*, *170*, *192*, *206*, 222, *224*
    See also specific principles
"Emotional Ability and Nonverbal Communication in Psychology and Marketing" study, 197
emotional intelligence, 196–198
emotions, 93
empathy, 198–200
employees, 27, 47–49, 86, 95–96, 105–107, 202, 211–212, 219
employers, 124–125
employment, 103–111
engineering, 64, 202
England, inns in, 37
etiquette, 89–91
excellence, demonstrating, 73

experience points, 54–56, 67
See also specific points
experiences, creating, 52–53

F
farewells, importance of, 66–67
feedback, 67–68, 94
finance/accounting departments, 65
first contacts, 56–57
first impressions, 58
fitness centeres, 58
follow-up, 56, 67–68
food/beverage (F&B) areas, 59–60, 214–215
forward thinking, 74
France, inns in, 37

G
Gardner, William, 214
gift shops, 58
goals, 141–143
Golder, P. N., 80
Goleman, Daniel, 197
guest mindsets, 76–79
guest rooms, 55, 64, 211
guests, 63, 164, 216–218
   engaging, 54–55, 76–77
   first impressions of, 58
   and food/beverage areas, 59
   surprising, 77
   unhappy, 78, 94–95

H
handwriting, 196
Hasford, Jonathan, 197
heart of the house, 63–66
higher education, 229–232, 234–235
    Doctorate, 236–238
    EMBA, 230–231, 234, 236
hospitality, 41, 48–49
    defining, 35–36
    personal characteristics of, 7–8, *122*, 159, *160*
hosting/entertaining, family experiences with, 69–72
hotel lobby, 57, 77
hotel restaurants, 60, 77–78, 232
hotel schools, 21, 100–101, 105–106, 234
    See also École Hôtelière de Lausanne (EHL)
hoteliers, 35–36, 71
    characteristics of, 74–84
    defining, 72–73, 85–86
    dressing the part, 87–88
    personality, 16–17
    role of, 54, 71
hotels, 47, 50, 211, 232
    applying for employment, 103–104
    author's early experiences with, 16
    compared with stages, 10, 132
    consolidation of, 103
    employing, 106–107
    facilities, 41–42
    grand hotels, 37–38
    historical milestones, 44–46
    luxury, 48–49
    origins, 35

wi-fi, 45
"hotels of tomorrow", 42
housekeeping, 55, 63–64, 211–212
human resources departments, 65–66, 225–226
humility, 162
Hyatt Hotels, 45

I
India, 41
industrial revolution, 38
initiative, importance of, 10–11
innovation, 43–44, 182–183, 232
intangible rewards, 50
integrity, 161
internet, 45
interviewing, 26–28, 104–109
iPads, 45
Italy, Le Danieli, 38

J
Japan, 37
    Henn-na Hotel, 45
Jing, G., 151
judging, 194

K
Kalin, N. H., 199
Kidwell, Blair, 197

L
Lascaux caves, 36
laundry, 55, 63–64

leadership, 10, 167, 207
   authentic, 213–217, 221
   author as housekeeping manager, 29, 212–213
   and corporate culture, 152–153, 156–157
   and example, 86–87, 92
   learning for, 103
   and orchestras, 18
   responsibilities of, 10, 52, 65, 73, 81
   servant, 210–213, 217, 221
   styles, *122*, 205, *206*
   support from, 124
   transactional, 216–219
   transformational, 217, 219–221
   vs. management, 207–210
   and working environments, 211–212
Leroy, Hannes, 214
Levy-Bonvin, Jacques, "Hotels: A Brief History", 36
L'Hotel des Trois Rois (Switzerland), 37
listening, 200–202
local patrons, 59
looking ahead, 74
lost luggage, 79
luxury hotels, 48–49, 78

M
Ma, Jack, 42, 45, 184
Malcolm Baldridge Quality Award, 81
management, vs. leadership, 207–210
managers, and motivation, 135
manners, 89–91
marketing/public relations staff, 63
Marriott, Bill, 156

Marriott International, 46, 185
Marriott, John Willard, 156, 161
MBA classes, 230–232
meetings, 174–176, 178
  See also presentations
memory-creation, 62, 75, 79, 81
memory moments (MMs), 74–76, 215
mentorship, 22–23, 113–115
Middle Ages, 37
Middle East, travel to, 40
mission statements, 139, *140*, 146
  corporate, 154–155
mistakes, 21, 141
Mitra, D., 80
mobile technology, 185
Moorman, C., 80
music, 18–19, 132, 177–178

N
names, and discretion, 58
Nitschke, J. B., 199
non-verbal communication, 193–194
Nordstrom, 184–185
note-taking, 114–115

O
on-the-job training, 226–227
online booking, 45
optimism, 162–163, 167
organizations, and mentorship, 114–115
orientations, importance of, 21

255

P
patience, 166–167
people, 74–75, 240
"people businesses", 49–50
"People first!" slogan, 156, 161
people-oriented management, 151
people professionals, 54, 58, 61–62, 74–75, 89
people skills, improving, 60–61
personal brands, 111–112, *122*, 127, *128*, 129, 131–137, 144
personal core values, 130
personal grooming, 87–88
personal growth, 32–33, 111, 115, 117, 123–125, 171, 225, 228–229
   See also continuing education
personal statements, 136, 143–145
Pinho, J. C., 152
Pizzagalli, D., 198–199
planning, 172–174
presentations, 176–181
   See also meetings
Promus Hotel Corporation, 45
public areas, 55, 57–58

Q
quality, 81
   defining, 79–80
quality mindset, 79–82
questions
   about benefits, 107
   about yourself, 112, 129–130, 136
   and critical thinking, 187
   and mission statements, 155

R

relay stations, 54–55
repeat business, 71
reservations, 55–57
resorts, 40
respect, earning, 129
restrooms, 78
Ritz-Carlton, 28–29, 81
Ritz, César, 39, 113, 232
Rodrigues, A. P., 152
role models, 113–114, 228
roles, understanding, 91–92
Romans, in Baden, 36–37
room service, 44–45, 233
Rooms Division, 58–59
rudeness, 27

S

salaries, 107–108
sales/marketing division, 63
sales team, 63
Schulze, Horst, 29
Schwartz, Mark, 152
self-improvement, 161, 222
senses tests, 62
servant leadership, 210–213, 217, 221
service
    importance of, 51
    superior, 75
service professions, requirements of, 51
setbacks, 134
Shangri-La Hotels and Resorts Group, 41

Silk Road, 37
skills, developing, 131–132, 134, 177
smartphones, 46
smiles, 50, 88
social media, 59, 171
spas, 58
Statler, E. M., 39
stories, your own, 132–133, 135
strategizing, 84
success, 22, 134–135, 141–142, 230
Swiss watch metaphor, 53, 81
Switzerland, 39
   Baden, 15, 36–37
   Badrutt's Palace, 39
   Basel, 37
   Baur au Lac, 38
   Gstaad Palace, 39
   Lake Geneva, 101
   L'Hôtel des Bergues, 38
   L'Hotel des Trois Couronnes, 38
   L'Hotel des Trois Rois, 37

T
tailoring, process of, 80
talents, 131
   nurturing, 22
teaching moments, 94
teams, 182–183
teamwork, 53–55
technological improvements, 233
TED Talks, 181
thermal baths, 36–37

time management, 172–174
tonality art, 193
tourism, 39–40
training, importance of, 20
transactional leadership, 216–219
transformational leadership, 217, 219–221

U
United States
    Boston Park Plaza, 39, 44
    City Hotel, New York, 38
    Holt Hotel, 44
    Malcolm Baldridge Quality Award, 81
    Palmer House Hotel, 44
    rail lines, 38
    Roosevelt Hotel, 39, 45
    Tremont House, 44
    Waldorf Astoria, 44

V
virtual reality, 45–46, 233
vision, 146
    defining, 139, *140*
    executive need for, 141
visualization, 32–33

W
welcome, lack of, 26–27
Westin Hotel Group, 45
"What Is Quality?" study, 80
wi-fi, 45
word-of-mouth, 71

work/life balances, 116–118, 230–231
working environments, and leadership, 211–212
written communication, 195–196

ABOUT THE AUTHOR

Iwan Dietschi, "Dr. Hotelier," is an internationally trained Swiss executive with more than twenty-eight years of luxury hotel experience, mostly with Ritz-Carlton around the world. He has been involved in more than twenty hotel openings of The Ritz-Carlton and other luxury brands of Marriott International throughout four continents. A natural teacher, role model, and constant innovator, he has a passion for mentoring the next generation of hotel and hospitality leaders and is a frequent speaker at various business schools and industry events. Dr. Dietschi received his Doctor of Business Administration from the College of Management and Technology at Walden University (USA) and his Executive MBA from California State University, Monterey Bay, in 2012. He is a graduate of the world-renowned École Hôtelière de Lausanne (Switzerland).

www.ingramcontent.com/pod-product-compliance
Ingram Content Group UK Ltd.
Pitfield, Milton Keynes, MK11 3LW, UK
UKHW040618080525
5824UKWH00006B/10/J